PRESENTED TO

PRESENTED BY

DATE

Everything Romance
Published by WaterBrook Press
12265 Oracle Boulevard, Suite 200
Colorado Springs, Colorado 80921

ISBN 978-0-307-72931-6
ISBN 978-0-307-72932-3 (electronic)

Compiled by Todd Hafer and Rebecca Currington in association with Snapdragon Group℠, Tulsa, Oklahoma, USA.

Cover design by Thinkpen Design Inc.

Published in the United States by WaterBrook Multnomah, an imprint of the Crown Publishing Group, a division of Random House Inc., New York.

WaterBrook and its deer colophon are registered trademarks of Random House Inc.

Printed in the United States of America
2011—First Edition

10 9 8 7 6 5 4 3 2 1

Special Sales
Most WaterBrook Multnomah books are available at special quantity discounts when purchased in bulk by corporations, organizations, and special-interest groups. Custom imprinting or excerpting can also be done to fit special needs. For information, please e-mail SpecialMarkets@WaterBrookMultnomah.com or call 1-800-603-7051.

Everything Romance

WaterBrook
PRESS

All that we love deeply becomes a part of us.

HELEN KELLER

A Marriage Blessing

Most gracious God, we give You thanks for Your tender love in sending Jesus Christ to come among us, to be born of a human mother, and to make the way of the cross to be the way of life.

We thank You, also, for consecrating the union of man and woman in His name. By the power of Your Holy Spirit, pour out the abundance of Your blessing upon this man and this woman. Defend them from every enemy. Lead them into all peace. Let their love for each other be a seal upon their hearts, a mantle about their shoulders, and a crown upon their foreheads. Bless them in their work and in their companionship; in their sleeping and in their waking; in their joys and in their sorrows; in their life and in their death. Finally, in Your mercy, bring them to that table where Your saints feast forever in Your heavenly home; through Jesus Christ our Lord, who with You and the Holy Spirit, lives and reigns, one God, forever and ever.

Amen.

from *The Book of Common Prayer*

PERFECT PAIR
PIZZA-PITA SNACKS

2 whole-wheat pita breads
4 teaspoons basil pesto
1 cup cottage cheese
2 tablespoons Roma tomatoes, chopped
2 teaspoons fresh basil, chopped
Fresh Parmesan cheese (optional)

Toast pita breads until they are crispy and firm. Spread half of the pesto on each pita. Next, spread half of the cottage cheese on each pita. Top with chopped tomato and fresh basil. If desired, sprinkle with fresh grated parmesan cheese. Slice each pita into two or four wedges and enjoy!

Romance Trivia

A team of medical experts in Virginia contends that you're more likely to catch the common cold virus by shaking hands than by kissing.

TRADITIONAL WEDDING ANNIVERSARY GIFTS BY YEAR

According to tradition, there are specific kinds of gifts you should give your spouse each year. Start with the traditional gift, and give it a creative touch to make it your own. The key word when it comes to anniversary gifts is *thoughtful* rather than *extravagant*.

First Anniversary The traditional gift for the first year is paper. Consider a homemade card, a photo, or even a framed copy of your marriage certificate.

Second Anniversary The traditional gift for the second year is cotton. Choose a set of Egyptian cotton sheets that you can both enjoy or a cotton rope hammock you can both relax in on a lazy afternoon. Or buy each other a luxurious cotton robe.

Fifth Anniversary The traditional gift for the fifth year is wood. A wooden plaque, jewelry box, cigar box, or piece of furniture are popular choices.

Tenth Anniversary The traditional gift for ten years is tin or aluminum. Choose jewelry or a decorative object, such as a photo album. If you're in a more creative mood, plan a trip or getaway and travel by boat or plane (both made partially of aluminum and tin).

Twentieth Anniversary The traditional gift for year twenty is china. Get a commemorative china plate with your wedding date on it or a china figurine.

Thirtieth Anniversary The traditional gift for year thirty is pearl. This can be anything from a lovely strand of pearls to a night together at an oyster bar.

Fortieth Anniversary The traditional gift for year forty is ruby. Not only would jewelry be appropriate, but also any type of ruby-colored clothing.

Fiftieth Anniversary The traditional gift for year fifty is gold. Gold-plated home accents, jewelry, or memory keepsakes are all popular choices.

Sixtieth Anniversary The traditional gift for year sixty is the most prized of all—diamonds. A diamond-studded watch, diamond-encrusted picture frame, or piece of diamond jewelry are all great choices. Be creative and choose something that fits your own personal style.

A Prayer of Thanks for Our Marriage

Dear Loving Creator,

Thank You for our marriage, a unique relationship in the entire world—and for loving us personally. May we sense Your love and acceptance every day. Yes, we are a work in progress—that's for sure. But we are *your* work in progress.

Amen.

The Blue Dress

By Beatrice Fishback

The blue dress fluttered. I saw her move toward the boardwalk and hasten to the water's edge. I followed close behind. The waves licked her bare feet and kissed her toes as the blue dress wrapped around her hips and waist. I watched the back of her shoulders heave with gut-wrenching sobs. It was as if the waves had traveled over her feet, up her legs, through her body, and pushed their way out her throat. The strength and depth of her sorrow matched the water's power. The folds of the blue dress flapped up and down in the wind, but she seemed oblivious to it all.

He had loved that dress. I had overheard him tell her that many times. She would giggle and slide her arm into his, and they would dance around the kitchen to music only they could hear. Then she would rise on her toes like a ballerina and kiss his chin and cheek.

The beautiful blue dress. She wore it to meet him when he came home from the war on terror. Dressed in his uniform, he looked above the crowd to catch a glimpse of her. Was he worried she wouldn't be there? He should have known better. She pressed past the banners, pushed others aside, raced to his arms, and jumped into his embrace. She clung to him as if she would never let go. Finally, she released her embrace, and they held each other's hands and gazed into each other's eyes as if no one else were alive. They were afloat on a sea of love, and they would travel together to worlds known only to them. I stood by and watched.

But then he went away again. The war continued, and our country needed him as much as the woman he loved. She took him to the airport and waved as his figure disappeared into the cave of the aircraft. The door closed, and he sat at the window and placed a hand on the windowpane. I saw his lips form the words "I love you."

The plane lifted, and he was gone. She never saw him again. They said he died a hero.

She slipped the blue dress on. She combed her hair and brushed a dash of color onto her lips. I didn't really understand what was going on. What happened to the dancing in the kitchen? What happened to their warm embraces? We walked together down the long aisle of the church, and many people gathered around us. Some hugged and cried; others sat in stillness.

Later we stood at the water's edge. Her shoulders lifted up with her sorrow, and tears streamed down her clear pale skin. She peered and strained to look past the water, as if searching the sky for him to appear. Perhaps she expected him to walk toward her. Perhaps it had all just been a terrible dream. Finally, she took my hand. As we walked away, she said, "Your daddy is not coming home anymore, and I know you will miss him just as much as I do."

Later, her blue dress lay folded on the bed. She would never wear it again. Many years have passed, but I will always remember the love of my father and how he spoke of his love to my mother. I can still see him dancing with her to the music in the kitchen. Music only they could hear. And I can still see his face when his eyes found her in the crowd. And, oh, how he loved her beautiful blue dress.[1]

PERFECT PAIR
ROBERT BROWNING
AND ELIZABETH BARRETT

Prior to their marriage, Victorian poets Robert and Elizabeth Browning courted via letters—because Elizabeth's father disapproved of Robert, whom he regarded as too poor and low class for his daughter. In fact, he vowed to cut off all communication with his daughter if their romance continued.

The duo's letters, written over a courtship of almost two years, number almost six hundred and are among the world's most famous love letters. These letters reflect a love that wouldn't be denied: Even though Elizabeth's family eventually disowned her, she would go on to marry Robert, her true love. The marriage lasted for fifteen years, until the day Elizabeth died, cradled in Robert's arms.

From "The Love Chapter"

If I speak in the tongues of mortals and of angels, but do not have love, I am a noisy gong or a clanging symbol. And if I have prophetic powers, and understand all mysteries and all knowledge, and if I have all faith, so as to remove mountains, but do not have love, I am nothing. If I give away all my possessions, and if I hand over my body so that I may boast, but do not have love, I gain nothing.

Love is patient; love is kind; love is not envious or boastful or arrogant or rude. It does not insist on its own way; it is not irritable or resentful; it does not rejoice in wrongdoing, but rejoices in the truth. It bears all things, believes all things, hopes all things, endures all things.

Love never ends.

1 Corinthians 13:1–8, NRSV

You "Compete" Me!

Assuming that "friendly competition" is NOT an oxymoron for you and your beloved, a good-natured contest can be a lot of fun. You can pick an activity that both of you are skilled in, or see who is top dog at a new and unfamiliar competition for the both of you. (In fact, if you are both ultracompetitive, it might be wise to opt for a sport or activity that neither of you has done before—or at least not in a long while. For example, if you are both competitive tennis players, stay off the court and opt for a round of miniature golf.)

You can raise the stakes a bit by agreeing on a prize for the winner: the loser buys dessert, the winner gets to pick the next movie you see together, the winner gets a massage, and so on.

Cost: This is a great date for the budget conscious. A tennis match at a local park or a game of H-O-R-S-E on an outdoor basketball court at a nearby school costs you nothing. The same with a mile race at a track or on a park path. You might even be able to walk to your competition site. Low-cost options include a game of miniature golf, an informal video-game tournament at a nearby arcade, or a couple of rounds in a batting cage.

Make the Date Deluxe: You might want to add an element of "officiality" to your competition. For example, you can both sign up for a local five-kilometer road race. Train together and see who ends up being fastest on race day. If one of you is a clearly superior runner, add a "time handicap" to the faster runner's finishing time. Or, base the competition on who finishes higher among one's gender and/or age group. Or, sign up for a coed softball league and determine a winner based on highest batting average for the season.

Resources: Your local Parks and Recreation department's website should provide a wide range of options. And check out the calendar and sports sections of your local paper.

As I tell you repeatedly, you cannot possibly know what you mean to me. The days I do not see you are merely so many obstacles to be got over somehow before I see you. Each night as I go to bed, I sigh with relief because I am one day nearer to you. So it has been this week, and it is only Monday that I was with you. Today I am jubilant, and my work goes well. And I am saying to myself all the time, "Tonight I shall see her! Tonight I shall see her!"

FROM AUTHOR JACK LONDON
TO HIS WIFE, CHARMIAN KITTREDGE

WEDDING PROJECTILES FROM AROUND THE WORLD

American weddings feature the tossing of rice or birdseed, but here are the projectiles of choice for weddings in other parts of the world:

Turkey: candy
North Africa: figs and dates
France: wheat
Italy: coins, candy, and dried fruit
Greece: candied almonds
Former Czech Republic: dried peas
Mexico: red beads
Korea: nuts and dates
India: flower petals and puffed rice

*The greatest happiness in life is the conviction
that we are loved—loved for ourselves,
or rather, loved in spite of ourselves.*

VICTOR HUGO

Summum Bonum

All the breath and the bloom of the year in the bag of one bee:

All the wonder and wealth of the mine in the heart of one gem:

In the core of one pearl all the shade and the shine of the sea:

Breath and bloom, shade and shine—wonder, wealth,

and—how far above them—

Truth, that's brighter than gem,

Trust, that's purer than pearl—

Brightest truth, purest trust in the universe—all were for me

In the kiss of one girl.

Robert Browning

Did You Know? Frances Cleveland was the first bride of a U.S. president to be married in the White House. Additionally, the twenty-one-year-old's marriage to Grover Cleveland made her the youngest-ever First Lady. Seven years later, Frances gave birth to Esther Cleveland, the only child ever born to a First Lady in the White House.

Be patient with each other, making allowance for
each other's faults because of your love.

EPHESIANS 4:2, NLT

May your unfailing love rest upon us,
O LORD, even as we put our hope in you.

PSALM 33:22, NIV

Naomi said, "Look, your sister-in-law is going back
home to live with her own people and gods; go with her."
But Ruth said, "Don't force me to leave you; don't make
me go home. Where you go, I go; and where you live,
I'll live. Your people are my people, your God is my god;
where you die, I'll die, and that's where I'll be buried, so
help me God—not even death itself is going to come
between us!" When Naomi saw that Ruth had her heart
set on going with her, she gave in. And so the two of
them traveled on together to Bethlehem.

RUTH 1:15–18

How to Love for a Lifetime

Say "I love you" every day.
For best results, repeat yourself.

Treat each other with respect.

Keep confidences.

Know when to keep your mouth shut.

Look for the best in each other.

Laugh together. Private jokes are encouraged.

Find at least one common interest.

Be honest about your feelings.

When you're being honest, also be kind.

Have eyes only for each other.

One word: patience.

A little loyalty goes a long way.

Understand that the feelings
of love ebb and flow.

Never give up on the two of you.

Always give the benefit of the doubt.

Don't keep secrets–unless they're surprises!

Affection is not a personal choice;
it's a marriage must.

Be quick to forgive.

Leave the past in the past.

Avoid assumptions.

Eat at least one meal together every day.

Treat each other like special guests
in your home.

Put God first and each other second.

Be willing to learn from each other.

Pray together every day.

Anniversary Trivia

Even though there is no record of anyone ever celebrating

their one hundredth anniversary, it is listed on the

Anniversary Gift List as a ten-carat diamond.

Special Occasion Gift Idea

Every year, men and women buy jewelry for anniversaries, birth-days, and Valentine's Day. Then they present their sweethearts with overpriced rings, necklaces, bracelets, and earrings. Instead, shop antique stores and look for pieces with classic style and character. The only caveat is that your piece should have gold-plated or silver mountings. Odds are good you'll come away with something really beautiful without emptying your checking account or overloading your charge card.

Romance Trivia

Studies indicate that a man who kisses his wife good-bye
when he leaves for work every morning averages a higher
income than those who don't. Husbands who exercise
the rituals of affection tend to be more painstaking, more
stable, more methodical, and thus, higher earners. Studies
also show that men who kiss their wives before leaving in
the morning live five years longer than those who don't.

*Put your hand on a hot stove for a minute
and it seems like an hour; sit with
a pretty woman for an hour and it
seems like a minute. That's relativity.*

ALBERT EINSTEIN

Ten Things a Couple Can Make, Besides Money

1. Time
2. Merry
3. Do
4. Up
5. Sense

6. Peace
7. Room
8. Waves
9. Love
10. Believe

COUPLES LOOK GOOD IN GREEN!

More and more of today's couples are becoming environmentally conscious. They want to care for the planet, and couples with children want to set a good example of environmental stewardship. But did you know that "being green" can also help you keep out of the red? And it's a great way to save money for more romantic things, like dates, vacations, and gifts. Here are some tips on how you and your family can be green *and* save some green at the same time!

Wash clothes in cold water. Doing a load of laundry via a hot-water wash and warm rinse costs five to ten times more than a cold wash and rinse. And you can be even greener by reducing the amount of detergent you use in each load. (Use three-fourths or two-thirds of a cup instead of a full cup.) You'll save money and reduce the pollution of fresh water.

Recycle. Recycling reduces the amount of garbage that is burned or discarded to landfills. Don't think that one couple or family can make a difference here? Think again. Recycling just *one* aluminum can saves enough electricity to light a 100-watt bulb for 3.5 hours. And you save a pound of carbon for every ten glass bottles you recycle. By the way, if you don't see enough (or any) recycling bins around your town, make some noise about it.

Use a double-sided printer. This move, of course, means buying half as much paper. (And even if your personal printer isn't double-sided, there's a good chance the one at work—or the kids' school—could be.) Another tip: Use a printer's "draft" setting whenever possible. In one test, a typical inkjet printed twelve pages per minute in regular mode, but thirty-six ppm on the draft setting.

Replace incandescent bulbs with compact fluorescent bulbs. The new compact bulbs help fight climate change by reducing the fossil fuels that are burned. Over the life of just one bulb, you save one hundred pounds of carbon—for each incandescent bulb that is replaced by a compact fluorescent. These bulbs are more expensive than the traditional ones, of course, but they last longer, so you save on replacement costs—and maybe reduce trips to the store to boot.

BYOC (Bring Your Own Cup). Bring your own drinking cup or mug to work or meetings at the coffee shop. Doing this every day saves about twenty-three pounds of waste annually.

Skimp your ride. If possible, ride a bike, walk, or take public transportation to work, the store, etc. You'll save about $1,400 a year in gas (plus even more in oil and other "vital fluids"). You'll extend the life of your vehicle because you're putting less wear and tear on it, and you may reduce your time on the road with all those crazy drivers. The type of public-transportation vehicles used varies from city to city, but this mode of transportation typically produces between 50 and 95 percent fewer emissions per mile than private vehicles. Public transportation also frees you up to (safely!) read, make phone calls, catch up on e-mail, text message, or eat. So you can be more efficient while you help the environment.

Drive smart. There are a host of things you can do here. Obeying the speed limit conserves your gas—your expensive gas. For example, for every mile-per-hour you exceed 55 mph, you decrease your fuel economy by 1 percent. Want to improve your miles-per-gallon even more? Drive smoothly. Strive for easy acceleration and braking—look ahead to anticipate turns, hills, and stoplights. This style of driving is safer, and it reduces wear on your engine, transmission, and brakes. Speaking of wear, you can protect your tires by inflating them to the proper psi. Your car will handle better, and your mileage will improve, too. And don't let your car idle unnecessarily. Kill the engine while you're waiting in a friend's driveway, a parking lot, or your bank's drive-up window or ATM. When your car is idling, your mpg's drop to zero, but your car continues to generate greenhouse gases.

If you need a little incentive to adopt the above habits, consider this: If you can improve your car's mpg from fifteen to twenty, you'll save two hundred gallons of gas a year (based on twelve thousand miles driven). If gas is three bucks a gallon, that's an extra six hundred dollars in your pocket every year.

Love Buster
Dispense with the small showings of affection, hand holding, and cheek kissing. Those are just for the newly in love, right?

The woman's vision is deep reaching,
the man's far reaching. With the man
the world is his heart, with the woman
the heart is her world.

BETTY GRABLE

The slowest kiss makes too much haste.

THOMAS MIDDLETON

The quarrels of lovers are the renewal of love.

TERENCE

My husband and I have figured out a
really good system about the housework:
Neither one of us does it.

DOTTIE ARCHIBALD

Prayer of Any Husband

Lord, may there be no moment in her life
When she regrets that she became my wife,
And keep her dear eyes just a trifle blind
To my defects, and to my failings kind!

Help me to do the utmost that I can
To prove myself her measure of a man,
But, if I often fail as mortals may,
Grant that she never sees my feet of clay!

And let her make allowance now and then—
That we are only grown-up boys, we men,
So, loving all our children, she will see,
Sometimes, a remnant of the child in me!

Since years must bring to all their load of care,
Let us together every burden bear,
And when Death beckons one its path along,
May not the two of us be parted long!

MAZIE V. CARUTHERS

"YOU BET I LOVE YOU" CHOCOLATE-COVERED STRAWBERRIES

16 ounces milk, semisweet, or dark chocolate chips
2 tablespoons shortening, such as Crisco (oil or
   butter won't work)
1 carton of big, ripe strawberries
4 ounces of white chocolate chips, optional

Place chocolate chips in a double boiler and melt slowly. Add shortening and blend into the melted chips. Be careful not to get water in the chocolate.

Wash and dry the strawberries. Place a skewer or toothpick in the leafy end of the strawberry. Dip the strawberry half-way into the chocolate. Pull it out of the chocolate, and swirl it to eliminate drips. Place on parchment or waxed paper, and chill in the refrigerator for at least one hour.

To add an extra touch, melt the white chocolate chips and drizzle over the chilled strawberries. Yield: 12 strawberries.

For marriage to be a success, every woman and every man should have her or his own bathroom. The end.

CATHERINE ZETA-JONES

Love is friendship set to music.

JOSEPH CAMPBELL

There is one person I don't want to be angry at me, and her name is Ibis Cardenas Guillen, because if she gets angry at me, it's going to cost me a lot of money. My wife. Everybody else, I couldn't care less if they like me.

OZZIE GUILLEN

If you absolutely must have the last word in all marital spats, how about making it, "Sorry."

REV. ROBERT ST. JOHN

The Gift of the Magi

BY O. HENRY

One dollar and eighty-seven cents. That was all. And sixty cents of it was in pennies. Pennies saved one and two at a time by bull-dozing the grocer and the vegetable man and the butcher until one's cheeks burned with the silent imputation of parsimony that such close dealing implied. Three times Della counted it. One dollar and eighty-seven cents. And the next day would be Christmas.

There was clearly nothing to do but flop down on the shabby little couch and howl. So Della did it. Which instigates the moral reflection that life is made up of sobs, sniffles, and smiles, with sniffles predominating.

While the mistress of the home is gradually subsiding from the first stage to the second, take a look at the home. A furnished flat at $8 per week. It did not exactly fit beggar description, but it certainly had that word on the lookout for the mendicancy squad.

In the vestibule below was a letter-box into which no letter would go, and an electric button from which no mortal finger could coax a ring. Also appertaining thereunto was a card bearing the name "Mr. James Dillingham Young."

The "Dillingham" had been flung to the breeze during a former period of prosperity when its possessor was being paid $30 per week. Now, when the income was shrunk to $20, the letters of "Dillingham" look blurred, as though they were thinking seriously of contracting to a modest and unassuming D. But whenever Mr. James Dillingham Young came home and reached his flat above he was called "Jim" and greatly hugged by Mrs. James Dillingham Young, already introduced to you as Della. Which is all very good.

Della finished her cry and attended to her cheeks with the powder rag. She stood by the window and looked out dully at a gray cat walking a gray fence in a gray backyard. Tomorrow would be Christmas Day, and she had only $1.87 with which to buy Jim a present. She had been saving every penny she could for months, with this result. Twenty dollars a week doesn't go far. Expenses had been greater than she had calculated. They always are. Only $1.87 to buy a present for Jim. Her Jim. Many a happy hour she had spent planning for something nice for him. Something fine and rare and sterling—something just a little bit near to being worthy of the honor of being owned by Jim.

There was a pier-glass between the windows of the room. Perhaps you have seen a pier-glass in an $8 flat. A very thin and very agile person may, by observing his reflection in a rapid sequence of longitudinal strips, obtain a fairly accurate conception of his looks. Della, being slender, had mastered the art.

Suddenly she whirled from the window and stood before the glass. Her eyes were shining brilliantly, but her face had lost its color within twenty seconds. Rapidly she pulled down her hair and let it fall to its full length.

Now, there were two possessions of the James Dillingham Youngs in which they both took a mighty pride. One was Jim's gold watch that had been his father's and his grandfather's. The other was Della's hair. Had the Queen of Sheba lived in the flat across the airshaft, Della would have let her hair hang out the window some day to dry just to depreciate Her Majesty's jewels and gifts. Had King Solomon been the janitor, with all his treasures piled up in the basement, Jim would have pulled out his watch every time he passed, just to see him pluck at his beard from envy.

So now Della's beautiful hair fell about her rippling and shining like a cascade of brown waters. It reached below her knee and made itself almost a garment for her. And then she did it up again nervously and quickly. Once she faltered for a minute and stood still while a tear or two splashed on the worn red carpet.

On went her old brown jacket; on went her old brown hat. With a whirl of skirts and with the brilliant sparkle still in her eyes, she fluttered out the door and down the stairs to the street.

Where she stopped the sign read: "Mme. Sofronie. Hair Goods of All Kinds." One flight up Della ran, and collected herself, panting. Madame, large, too white, chilly, hardly looked the "Sofronie."

"Will you buy my hair?" asked Della.

"I buy hair," said Madame. "Take yer hat off and let's have a sight at the looks of it."

Down rippled the brown cascade.

"Twenty dollars," said Madame, lifting the mass with a practiced hand.

"Give it to me quick," said Della.

Oh, and the next two hours tripped by on rosy wings. Forget the hashed metaphor. She was ransacking the stores for Jim's present.

She found it at last. It surely had been made for Jim and no one else. There was no other like it in any of the stores, and she had turned all of them inside out. It was a platinum fob chain simple and chaste in design, properly proclaiming its value by substance alone and not by meretricious ornamentation—as all good things should do. It was even worthy of The Watch. As soon as she saw it she knew that it must be Jim's. It was like him. Quietness and value—the description applied to both. Twenty-one dollars they took from her for it, and she hurried home with the 87 cents. With that chain on his watch Jim might be properly anxious about the time in any company. Grand as the watch was, he sometimes looked at it on the sly on account of the old leather strap that he used in place of a chain.

When Della reached home her intoxication gave way a little to prudence and reason. She got out her curling irons and lighted the gas and went to work repairing the ravages made by generosity added to love. Which is always a tremendous task, dear friends—a mammoth task.

Within forty minutes her head was covered with tiny, close-lying curls that made her look wonderfully like a truant school-boy. She looked at her reflection in the mirror long, carefully, and critically.

"If Jim doesn't kill me," she said to herself, "before he takes a second look at me, he'll say I look like a Coney Island chorus girl. But what could I do—oh! What could I do with a dollar and eighty-seven cents?"

At 7 o'clock the coffee was made and the frying-pan was on the back of the stove hot and ready to cook the chops.

Jim was never late. Della doubled the fob chain in her hand and sat on the corner of the table near the door that he always entered. Then she heard his step on the stairway down on the first flight, and she turned white for just a moment. She had a habit of saying little silent prayers about the simplest everyday things, and now she whispered: "Please God, make him think I am still pretty."

The door opened and Jim stepped in and closed it. He looked thin and very serious. Poor fellow, he was only twenty-two—and to be burdened with a family! He needed a new overcoat and he was without gloves.

Jim stopped inside the door, as immovable as a setter at the scent of quail. His eyes were fixed upon Della, and there was an expression in them that she could not read, and it terrified her. It was not anger, nor surprise, nor disapproval, nor horror, nor any of the sentiments that she had been prepared for. He simply stared at her fixedly with that peculiar expression on his face.

Della wriggled off the table and went for him.

"Jim, darling," she cried, "don't look at me that way. I had my hair cut off and sold it because I couldn't have lived through Christmas without giving you a present. It'll grow out again—you won't mind, will you? I just had to do it. My hair grows awfully fast. Say 'Merry Christmas!' Jim, and let's be happy. You don't know what a nice—what a beautiful, nice gift I've got for you."

"You've cut off your hair?" asked Jim, laboriously, as if he had not arrived at that patent fact yet even after the hardest mental labor.

"Cut it off and sold it," said Della. "Don't you like me just as well, anyhow? I'm me without my hair, ain't I?"

Jim looked about the room curiously.

"You say your hair is gone?" he said, with an air almost of idiocy.

"You needn't look for it," said Della. "It's sold, I tell you—sold and gone, too. It's Christmas Eve, boy. Be good to me, for it went for you. Maybe the hairs of my head were numbered," she went on with a sudden serious sweetness, "but nobody could ever count my love for you. Shall I put the chops on, Jim?"

Out of his trance Jim seemed quickly to wake. He enfolded his Della. For ten seconds let us regard with discreet scrutiny some inconsequential object in the other direction. Eight dollars a week or a million a year—what is the difference? A mathematician or a wit would give you the wrong answer. The magi brought valuable gifts, but that was not among them. This dark assertion will be illuminated later on.

Jim drew a package from his overcoat pocket and threw it upon the table.

"Don't make any mistake, Dell," he said, "about me. I don't think there's anything in the way of a haircut or a shave that could make me like my girl any less. But if you'll unwrap that package, you may see why you had me going a while at first."

White fingers and nimble tore at the string and paper. And then an ecstatic scream of joy; and then, alas! A quick feminine change to hysterical tears and wails, necessitating the immediate employment of all the comforting powers of the lord of the flat.

For there lay The Combs—the set of combs, side and back, that Della had worshipped for long in a Broadway window. Beautiful combs, pure tortoise shell, with jeweled rims—just the shade to wear in the beautiful vanished hair. They were expensive combs, she knew, and her heart had simply craved and yearned over them without the least hope of possession. And now, they were hers, but the tresses that should have adorned the coveted adornments were gone.

But she hugged them to her bosom, and at length she was able to look up with dim eyes and a smile and say: "My hair grows so fast, Jim!"

And then Della leaped up like a little singed cat and cried, "Oh, oh!"

Jim had not yet seen his beautiful present. She held it out to him eagerly upon her open palm. The dull precious metal seemed to flash with a reflection of her bright and ardent spirit.

"Isn't it a dandy, Jim? I hunted all over town to find it. You'll have to look at the time a hundred times a day now. Give me your watch. I want to see how it looks on it."

Instead of obeying, Jim tumbled down on the couch and put his hands under the back of his head and smiled.

"Dell," said he, "let's put our Christmas presents away and keep 'em a while. They're too nice to use just at present. I sold the watch to get the money to buy your combs. And now suppose you put the chops on."

The magi, as you know, were wise men—wonderfully wise men—who brought gifts to the Babe in the manger. They invented the art of giving Christmas presents. Being wise, their gifts were no doubt wise ones, possibly bearing the privilege of exchange in case of duplication. And here I have lamely related to you the uneventful chronicle of two foolish children in a flat who most unwisely sacrificed for each other the greatest treasures of their house. But in a last word to the wise of these days let it be said that of all who give gifts these two were the wisest. Of all who give and receive gifts, such as they are the wisest. Everywhere they are wisest. They are the magi.

The Four Ways God Answers a Couple's Prayer

1. No, not yet.

2. No, I love you both too much.

3. Yes, I thought you'd never ask.

4. Yes, and here's more!

ANNE LEWIS

SENSUOUS
STEAMED OYSTERS

3 tablespoons butter
1 cup milk
2 pints shucked oysters with liquid
1 teaspoon salt
$\frac{1}{2}$ teaspoon pepper
$\frac{1}{2}$ teaspoon chopped parsley

Melt butter in skillet or saucepan. Add milk and liquid from the oysters. Add salt, pepper, and parsley. Heat, but do not boil. Add oysters. Cook for 5 minutes or until the edges curl. Serve immediately. Yield: 4–6 servings.

Note: Oysters have always been considered a strong aphrodisiac. The infamous lover, Casanova, was said to indulge himself with fifty oysters every morning for breakfast.

Small Is the Trust When Love Is Green

Small is the trust when love is green
In sap of early years;
A little thing steps in between
And kisses turn to tears.

Awhile—and see how love be grown
In loveliness and power!
Awhile, it loves the sweets alone,
But next it loves the sour.

A little love is none at all
That wanders or that fears;
A hearty love dwells still at call
To kisses or to tears.

Such then be mine, my love to give,
And such be yours to take:
A faith to hold, a life to live,
For lovingkindness' sake:

Should you be sad, should you be gay,
Or should you prove unkind,
A love to hold the growing way
And keep the helping mind:

A love to turn the laugh on care

When wrinkled care appears,

And, with an equal will, to share

Your losses and your tears.

ROBERT LOUIS STEVENSON

Did You Know? John Tyler, America's tenth president, was the first chief executive to marry while in office. At the time he was sworn in as president in 1841, his first wife, Letitia Tyler, was an invalid due to a paralytic stroke she suffered in 1839. She died in 1842. Twenty-two months later, President Tyler married Julia Gardiner, whom portraits reveal as bearing a striking resemblance to the president's first wife. Julia served as First Lady for the final eight months of her husband's presidency, and the couple eventually had seven children together.

THE LOVE YOU SAVE

Stuck for a creative "love gift" for your sweetie? How about the gift of a romantic memory jar?

Label it "You and me forever!" or something similar.

Tie a bow around the top and put a note inside, with a message like,

> This is to capture our special romantic moments—
> the prize a certain someone won at the carnival,
> the ticket stubs from the night we saw our favorite play,
> the famous romantic love poem,
> a petal from the flowers in our wedding bouquet—
> our love memories.

Sign your name and place the jar somewhere it will be discovered. You can keep adding to the memories, in more ways than one, for years to come.

Love Booster
Dance together, even if it's just in the kitchen for a few minutes before breakfast.

Romance Trivia

Wild cabbage was traditionally recommended as an aphrodisiac. The list also includes oysters, chocolate, strawberries, carrots, bananas, almonds, licorice, vanilla, mustard, and asparagus.

Romance Trivia

It's reported that more than ten thousand marriages a year now are directly traceable to romances that begin during coffee breaks.

Wedding Trivia

The kiss that is given by the groom to the bride at the end of the wedding ceremony originates from the earliest times when the couple would actually make love for the first time under the eyes of half the village!

Wedding Trivia

In Pennsylvania, ministers are forbidden from performing marriages when either the bride or groom is drunk.

Did You Know? Men pay a Chicago-based company called Selective Search a minimum of $20,000 a year to set them up on dates. The company reports its efforts have led to 1,221 marriages—and 417 babies. Eighty-eight percent of the firm's clients meet their eventual spouse during the first nine months of participation. Selective Search, which is run by a former executive recruiter, boasts a database of more than 140,000 eligible women.

Did You Know? If you are a married person, you are part of an increasingly rare breed. According to the 2010 U.S. Census, only 52 percent of Americans are married—the lowest percentage on record. At the time of the 2000 Census, 57 percent of Americans were married.

Did You Know? In 2010, Cincinnati Reds starting pitcher Edinson Volquez was suspended for fifty games for testing positive for a performance-enhancing drug. An embarrassed Volquez ultimately revealed the source of the positive test—which had nothing to do with baseball: a prescription fertility medication to help him and his wife conceive.

Love to faults is always blind,
Always is to joy inclined,
Lawless, winged, and unconfined,
And breaks all chains from every mind.

WILLIAM BLAKE

We have lived and loved together
Through many changing years;
We have shared each other's gladness,
And wept each other's tears.

CHARLES JEFFERYS

Love is anterior to life
Posterior to death
Initial of creation, and
The exponent of breath.

EMILY DICKINSON

The Book of Love

A book can be a magical path to exploring thoughts, dreams, mysteries, and ideas. Or it can be just good escapist fun and entertainment. You never know what doors can be opened by a visit to a bookstore, library, or book fair. Pick a book that reflects a common interest, and take turns reading chapters or sections to each other. If you prefer audio books, go that route, and listen together, on a scenic drive in your car—or just about anywhere via MP3 player or portable sound system. Be sure to include time to discuss or reflect on what you've read or heard.

Cost: Almost any way you look at it, books are a bargain. Ink-on-paper and audio books are free from your local library. (Hint: If you want to read a current bestseller, most libraries have an online system that allows you to request books. Request the large-print edition of that bestseller, as the wait for these editions is often shorter than the original version or the audio book.) If you want to purchase a book and still save some money, check out your local used-book store.

Make the Date Deluxe: Join (or form) a book club. It can be a lot of fun to meet with a group of people to discuss a book that interests everyone involved. Of course, you and your spouse can form your own private book club for two. Set a regular meeting time and place, such as every Saturday morning at a local coffee shop or restaurant.

Resources: Local bookstores, libraries, and coffee shops often provide book-club information. Librarians and bookstore personnel are also wonderful resources for choosing a book that is ideal for a club.

I kiss you firmly a hundred times, embrace you tenderly and am sketching in my imagination various pictures in which you and I figure, and nobody and nothing else.

FROM RUSSIAN PLAYWRIGHT ANTON CHEKHOV
TO HIS WIFE, OLGA CHEKHOVA

To Jane

The keen stars were twinkling,

and the fair moon was rising among them,

Dear Jane.

The guitar was tinkling,

But the notes were not sweet

till you sung them again.

As the moon's soft splendour

O'er the faint cold starlight of Heaven

is thrown,

So your voice most tender

to the strings without soul had then given

its own.

PERCY BYSSHE SHELLEY

Did You Know? The day after comedian Jack Benny died, his wife, Mary, received a single red rose. The rosy deliveries continued for the rest of Mary's life—due to a provision that Jack included in his will.

We are most alive when we're in love.

JOHN UPDIKE

Familiar acts are beautiful through love.

PERCY BYSSHE SHELLEY

*Greater love hath no man than to attend
the Episcopal Church with his wife.*

PRESIDENT LYNDON B. JOHNSON

*Love is a fruit in season at all times,
and within reach of every hand.*

MOTHER TERESA

"TAKE ME TO HEAVEN" HONEY-FRIED FIGS

1 tablespoon butter
1 tablespoon honey
4 ripe figs halved lengthwise
Cream, whipped cream, yogurt, or ice cream

Melt butter and honey in a frying pan. Place the fig halves cut-side down in the pan. Cook until bubbling and figs start to brown. Serve with cream, whipped cream, yogurt, or ice cream on the side, if you like. Yield: 2 servings.

Note: From ancient times, honey and figs have been thought to trigger sexual desire. Just enough of this double-hitter and you and your sweetheart will both be "smokin' hot"!

Valentine Gift Idea

Your sweetheart will be expecting a gift on Valentine's Day, but what if you were to surprise him or her with a Valentine's gift on some other day of the year? Frankly, you will pay the highest possible price for flowers, cards, even dinner on the actual day, and you will have to put up with crowded restaurants, movie theaters, and other venues. But if you celebrated Valentine's Day on, say, February 10, you might well find it to be a much more satisfying experience.

Anniversary Trivia

Originally the diamond was listed as the gift for a seventy-fifth anniversary. However, in 1897, the Diamond Jubilee was celebrated in honor of the sixtieth year of Queen Victoria's reign. Since then, the diamond has been designated for the sixtieth anniversary.

Love doesn't make the world go round,
Love is what makes the ride worthwhile.

ELIZABETH BARRETT BROWNING

Love is like a tennis match;
you'll never win consistently until
you learn to serve well.

DAN P. HEROD

All you'll get from strangers is surface
pleasantry or indifference. Only someone
who loves you will criticize you.

JUDITH CRIST

If ever comes a day when we can't be together,
keep me in your heart, I'll stay there forever.

A. A. MILNE

Love is not leisure, it is work.

ANNA QUINDLEN

SEDUCTIVELY SWEET STRAWBERRY–KIWI JAM

3 cups fresh strawberries, hulled and quartered

3 fresh kiwis, peeled and finely chopped

1.75-ounce packet of powdered fruit pectin

1 tablespoon finely chopped ginger

1 tablespoon butter

1 tablespoon lemon juice

1 teaspoon shredded orange peel

Dash salt

5 cups sugar

Mash berries in a bowl. Combine berries, kiwi, pectin, ginger, butter, lemon juice, orange peel, and salt. Heat mixture at medium-high, stirring constantly until it comes to a full rolling boil. Add sugar. Return to boiling. Boil 60 seconds, stirring constantly. Remove from heat and skim off foam with a metal spoon. Ladle jam into sterilized half-pint canning jars. Leave $1/4$ inch of headspace. Wipe rims of jars and screw on lids. Process in a boiling-water canner for 5 minutes. Remove jars and cool on racks. Yield: 6 half-pint jars.

Romeo and Juliet

ADAPTED FROM WILLIAM SHAKESPEARE

Romeo Montague leaves the Capulet masquerade ball where he met and instantly fell in love with Juliet. Unable to forget the beautiful daughter of his family's sworn enemies, he returns to the Capulet house, where he hopes for another glimpse of the girl.

He leaps the wall of the orchard, located at the back of Juliet's house. Here he has not been long, ruminating on his new love, when Juliet appears above at a window, through which her great beauty seems to break like the light of the sun in the east; and the moon, which shines in the orchard with a faint light, appears to Romeo as if sick and pale with grief at the superior luster of this new sun.

"But, soft! What light through yonder window breaks? It is the east, and Juliet is the sun. Arise, fair sun, and kill the envious moon."

Juliet leans on the casement, with her hand upon her cheek. Romeo speaks again, "It is my lady, O, it is my love! O, that I were a glove upon her hand, that I might touch that cheek!"

Thinking herself alone, Juliet steps out onto the balcony and exclaims, "Ah me!"

Romeo, enraptured to hear her speak, responds softly, "O speak again, bright angel! For thou art as glorious to this night as a winged messenger of heaven."

She, not being aware of Romeo's presence, calls upon her lover by name: "O Romeo, Romeo! Wherefore art thou, Romeo? Deny thy father and refuse thy name, for my sake; or if thou wilt not, be but my sworn love, and I no longer will be a Capulet."

Romeo, hearing this encouragement, wishes to speak, but he wants to hear more.

The lady continues her passionate discourse by declaring that Romeo should put away that hated name Montague. "What's in a name?" she asks, "That which we call a rose by any other name would smell as sweet. O Romeo, doft thy name and take me."

At this loving word, Romeo can no longer keep silent. He bids her call him by another name—even "Love."

Juliet is alarmed to hear a man's voice in the garden, but then knows it to be Romeo's. She declares that he is in grave danger if any of her kinsmen should find him here; it would mean death to him, being a Montague.

"Alack," says Romeo, "there is more peril in your eyes than in twenty of their swords. Do you but look kindly upon me, lady, and I am proof against their enmity. Better my life should be ended by their hate, than that hated life should be prolonged to live without your love."

"How came you into this place," asks Juliet, "and by whose direction?"

"Love directed me."

A crimson blush comes over Juliet's face, unseen by Romeo by reason of the night. But he, being anxious that she exchange a vow of love with him that night, listens as his Juliet explains that she already has given him her vow of love before he requested it.

A cloud hides the moon, and Juliet's nurse calls for her to come to bed. From the vantage of her balcony, Juliet leans toward Romeo and whispers, "Good night, good night! Parting is such sweet sorrow, that I shall say good night till it be morrow."

Reaching up to his Juliet, Romeo pronounces a benediction, "Sleep dwell upon thine eyes, peace in thy breast! Would I were sleep and peace, so sweet to rest!"

The Prayer of Francis of Assisi for Those in Love

As you lose yourselves in each other's love, keep aware of how easy it will be to so love and enjoy each other that you shut out those who need you individually and together. Pray this prayer together:

> Lord, make us instruments of Thy peace.
> Where there is hate, may we bring love;
> Where offence, may we bring pardon;
> May we bring union in place of discord;
> Truth, replacing error;
> Faith, where once there was doubt;
> Hope, for despair;
> Light, where there was darkness;
> Joy to replace sadness.
> Make us not to so crave to be loved as to love.
> Help us to learn that in giving we may receive;
> In forgetting ourselves, we may find life eternal.

Top Five Guys' Pick-Up Lines
(in Church)

1. "Hey, baby, what's your spiritual gift?"

2. "No, this pew isn't saved, but I sure am!"

3. "This sermon's dull—wanna try to start 'The Wave'?"

4. "Do you know I can bench press an entire set of exhaustive Bible commentaries?"

5. "Do you have a brother named Gabriel— because I'm sure you're an angel!"

Did You Know? During a kiss, nerves carry sensation from the lips to the brain. The brain responds by releasing a "love potion" of sorts: oxytocin, which creates feelings of affection and attachment; dopamine, which produces feelings of pleasure; serotonin, which elevates the mood; and adrenaline, which increases the heart rate.

How Many Times

How many times do I love again?

Tell me how many beads there are

in a silver chain

of evening rain.

Unravelled from the tumbling main

And threading the eye of a yellow star—

So many times do I love again.

THOMAS LOVELL BEDDOES

Did You Know? The wife of stay-at-home dad Michael Thompson was content to let her husband mind the kids while she worked. However, Thompson ended up making a huge financial contribution to the family one memorable year. He won a million dollars in a fantasy-fishing contest.

The Song—Best of All Songs— Solomon's Song!

THE WOMAN

Kiss me—full on the mouth!

Yes! For your love is better than wine,

headier than your aromatic oils.

The syllables of your name murmur like a meadow brook.

No wonder everyone loves to say your name!

Take me away with you! Let's run off together!

An elopement with my King-Lover!

We'll celebrate, we'll sing,

we'll make great music.

Yes! For your love is better than vintage wine.

Everyone loves you—of course! And why not?...

THE MAN

You're so beautiful, my darling,

so beautiful, and your dove eyes are veiled

By your hair as it flows and shimmers,

like a flock of goats in the distance

streaming down a hillside in the sunshine.

Your smile is generous and full—

expressive and strong and clean.

Your lips are jewel red,

your mouth elegant and inviting,

your veiled cheeks soft and radiant.
The smooth, lithe lines of your neck
command notice—all heads turn in awe and admiration!
Your breasts are like fawns,
twins of a gazelle, grazing among the first spring flowers.

The sweet, fragrant curves of your body,
the soft, spiced contours of your flesh
Invite me, and I come. I stay
until dawn breathes its light and night slips away.
You're beautiful from head to toe, my dear love,
beautiful beyond compare, absolutely flawless....

You've captured my heart, dear friend.
You looked at me, and I fell in love.
One look my way and I was hopelessly in love!
How beautiful your love, dear, dear friend—
far more pleasing than a fine, rare wine,
your fragrance more exotic than select spices.
The kisses of your lips are honey, my love,
every syllable you speak a delicacy to savor.
Your clothes smell like the wild outdoors,
the ozone scent of high mountains.
Dear lover and friend, you're a secret garden,
a private and pure fountain.
Body and soul, you are paradise,
a whole orchard of succulent fruits—

Ripe apricots and peaches,
oranges and pears;
Nut trees and cinnamon,
and all scented woods;
Mint and lavender,
and all herbs aromatic;
A garden fountain, sparking and splashing,
fed by spring waters from the Lebanon mountains....

I went to my garden, dear friend, best lover!
breathed the sweet fragrance.
I ate the fruit and honey,
I drank the nectar and wine.

Celebrate with me, friends!
Raise your glasses—"To life! To love!"

THE WOMAN

My dear lover glows with health—
red-blooded, radiant!
He's one in a million.
There's no one quite like him!
My golden one, pure and untarnished,
with raven black curls tumbling across his shoulders.
His eyes are like doves, soft and bright,
but deep-set, brimming with meaning, like wells of water.
His face is rugged, his beard smells like sage,

His voice, his words, warm and reassuring.
Fine muscles ripple beneath his skin,
quiet and beautiful.
His torso is the work of a sculptor,
hard and smooth as ivory.
He stands tall, like a cedar,
strong and deep-rooted,
A rugged mountain of a man,
aromatic with wood and stone.
His words are kisses, his kisses words.
Everything about him delights me, thrills me
through and through!

That's my lover, that's my man.

THE MAN

Dear, dear friend and lover,
you're as beautiful as Tirzah, city of delights,
Lovely as Jerusalem, city of dreams,
the ravishing visions of my ecstasy.
Your beauty is too much for me—I'm in over my head.
I'm not used to this! I can't take it in.
Your hair flows and shimmers
like a flock of goats in the distance
streaming down a hillside in the sunshine.
Your smile is generous and full—
expressive and strong and clean.

Your veiled cheeks
are soft and radiant.

There's no one like her on earth,
never has been, never will be.
She's a woman beyond compare.
My dove is perfection,
Pure and innocent as the day she was born,
and cradled in joy by her mother.
Everyone who came by to see her
exclaimed and admired her—
All the fathers and mothers, the neighbors and friends,
blessed and praise her.

Shapely and graceful your sandaled feet,
and queenly your movement—
Your limbs are lithe and elegant,
the work of a master artist.
Your body is a chalice,
wine-filled.
Your skin is silken and tawny
like a field of wheat touched by the breeze.
Your breasts are like fawns,
twins of a gazelle.
Your neck is carved ivory, curved and slender.
Your eyes are wells of light, deep with mystery.
Quintessentially feminine!

Your profile turns all heads,
commanding attention.
The feelings I get when I see the high mountain ranges
—stirrings of desire, longings for the heights—
Remind me of you,
and I'm spoiled for anyone else!
Your beauty, within and without, is absolute,
dear lover, close companion.
You are tall and supple, like the palm tree,
and your full breasts are like sweet clusters of dates.
I say, "I'm going to climb that palm tree!
I'm going to caress its fruit!"
Oh yes! Your breasts
will be clusters of sweet fruit to me,
Your breath clean and cool like fresh mint,
your tongue and lips like the best wine.

THE WOMAN

Yes, and yours are, too—my love's kisses
flow from his lips to mine.
I am my lover's.
I'm all he wants. I'm all the world to him!
Come, dear lover—
let's tramp through the countryside.
Let's sleep at some wayside inn,
then rise early and listen to bird-song.
Let's look for wildflowers in bloom,

blackberry bushes blossoming white,
Fruit trees festooned
with cascading flowers.
And there I'll give myself to you,
my love to your love!

Love-apples drench us with fragrance,
fertility surrounds, suffuses us,
Fruits fresh and preserved
that I've kept and saved just for you, my love.

THE MAN

I found you under the apricot tree,
and woke you up to love.
Your mother went into labor under that tree,
and under that very tree she bore you.

THE WOMAN

Hang my locket around your neck,
wear my ring on your finger.
Love is invincible facing danger and death.
Passion laughs at the terrors of hell.
The fire of love stops at nothing—
it sweeps everything before it.
Flood waters can't drown love,
torrents of rain can't put it out.

Love can't be bought, love can't be sold—
it's not to be found in the marketplace....

THE MAN

King Solomon may have vast vineyards
in lush, fertile country,
Where he hires others to work the ground.
People pay anything to get in on that bounty.
But *my* vineyard is all mine,
and I'm keeping it to myself.
You can have your vast vineyards, Solomon,
you and your greedy guests!

Oh, lady of the gardens,
my friends are with me listening.
Let me hear your voice!

THE WOMAN

Run to me, dear lover.
Come like a gazelle.
Leap like a wild stag
on the spice mountains.

Song of Songs 1:1–4; 4:1–15; 5:1; 5:10–16;
6:4–9; 7; 8:5–8; 8:11–14

At one glance

I love you

With a thousand hearts.

MIHRI HATUN

Song: To Celia

Drink to me only with thine eyes,

and I will pledge with mine;

Or leave a kiss but in the cup,

and I'll not look for wine.

BEN JOHNSON

The sunlight clasps the earth

and the moonbeams kiss the sea:

What is all this sweet work worth

if thou kiss not me?

PERCY BYSSHE SHELLEY

Did You Know? On the eve of Saint Andrew's Day (November 30), it's tradition for a young Scottish woman to petition Saint Andrew for a husband. As a sign her request will be met, the woman may throw a shoe at a door in her home. If the shoe's toe ends up pointing toward the exit, it's a sign that the woman will leave home and marry within the year.

Or, the woman can peel a whole apple rind and toss the peel over her shoulder. If the rind forms a letter of the alphabet, it will be the first initial of her future groom.

Did You Know? If you've been to a wedding lately, you have probably seen a lot of lace. The presence of lace, ribbons, and other frills at weddings dates back to the Middle Ages. A knight of this era would ride into battle sporting a ribbon or scarf given to him by his "lady fair." (Incidentally, the word *lace* comes from a Latin term meaning "to ensnare.")

Did You Know? Of all U.S. states, Alaska has the highest ratio of unmarried men to unmarried women—sparking the famous local saying, "The odds are good, but the goods are odd."

Creative Ways to Say "I Love You!" (Without Actually Saying "I Love You"). Perfect for Texting!

"Let's cuddle, ASAP!"

"You and moi, ooh-la-la!"

"You rock my socks!"

"Can't spell 'us' without U!"

"I ❤ you!"

"I'm so lucky to have you to adore!"

"You're the best time my heart has ever had!"

"XOXO!"

"We're so good together!"

"So glad you're mine, and I'm yours!"

"I followed my heart; it led me to you."

"My favorite place to be is in your heart."

"I'm nuts about you!"

"When I'm beside you, I'm beside myself!"

"I found you, and it's finders keepers!"

"You are my sunshine and my starshine!"

"I have a forever crush on you!"

"Your love makes my world go 'round!"

"You + Me = A Perfect Pair."

"I like you…and then some!"

"I'm stuck on you!"

"I'm all yours!"

"I'm crazy about you!"

"When I think of you, my heart smiles."

"You're my eternal object of affection!"

"You're the music, melody, and meaning in my life."

"I just adore adoring you!"

"If love is a color, our love is a rainbow!"

"You are my everything."

"Yours is the sweetest face in all of Facebook!"

"I'm over the moon for you."

"I'm always here, there, anywhere for you!"

"I'd be lost without you."

"You've got it—and I want it!"

"I'm so grateful that you and I became US!"

"I'm your number-one, not-so-secret admirer!"

"You—I couldn't ask for more!"

"You're so sweet that I wanna Tweet!"

The greatest pleasure of life is love.

SIR WILLIAM TEMPLE

Life is so precious. Please, please, let's love one another, live each day, reach out to each other, be kind to each other.

JULIA ROBERTS

I can live without money, but I cannot live without love.

JUDY GARLAND

Brevity is the soul of lingerie.

DOROTHY PARKER

It is only with the heart that one can see rightly,
what is essential is invisible to the eye.

ANTOINE DE SAINT-EXUPÉRY

PERFECT PAIR
JENNIE AND JEFF SALMON

Jennie and Jeff Salmon are partners in coaching and in marriage. The duo coach the Ward Melville High School fencing teams in New York. Jennie has led her women's team to ten straight unbeaten seasons, while Jeff's men's team has enjoyed five perfect seasons. Over the past decade, the Salmons' combined record is 273–10, with forty-seven fencers sent to NCAA programs, including four All-Americans, so far.

When you are in love with someone,
you want to be near him all the time,
except when you are out buying things
and charging them to him.

MISS PIGGY

A Blessing for Him

May your fountain be blessed, and may you rejoice in the wife of your youth.... May you ever be intoxicated with her love.

PROVERBS 5:18–19, NIV

Wedding Trivia

In the rhyme "Something old, something new, something borrowed, something blue," "blue" is symbolic of the blood of royalty, since both the bride and the groom were once considered to be "royal" on their wedding day.

HOT AND SPICY GUACAMOLE

1¼ cups fresh or frozen shelled peas
2 ripe avocados, halved, pitted, and peeled
2 tablespoons lime juice
¼ cup finely chopped red onion
1 garlic clove, minced
2 tablespoons chopped cilantro
1 small jalapeño pepper, seeded and thinly sliced
Water (for boiling peas)

Bring a medium saucepan of salted water to boiling. Add peas and simmer for 1 minute. Drain and rinse with cold water. Drain again and cool.

Place avocados and lime juice in a medium-sized bowl. With a fork, mash avocados. Add peas, onion, garlic, cilantro, and pepper. Season to taste with salt. Place in serving bowl and serve immediately with chips of your choice.

Candidate for Love

"Jim Gibson is having a fundraiser tonight. Want to go?" asked my friend Adella, who was volunteering for Gibson's political campaign.

"You know I come from a long line of diehard members of the *other* party," I said.

"So what? Going is better than you moping around home alone."

She was right. I'd hardly been anywhere since I'd broken up with my boyfriend six months earlier.

Three hours later, we were at the meeting, and I had to admit that Jim Gibson had charisma.

"Isn't he wonderful?" Adella asked.

I shrugged. "It's all just hype. For instance, what does he really know about education? Look at this." I waved a leaflet I'd been handed.

Adella put her hand on my arm, but my voice rose. "I get tired of politicians spouting their thirty-second cures. Let him get in the trenches and see..."

Adella's gaze had strayed over my shoulder. Was I *that* boring?

"And what trenches are we speaking about?" a voice behind me said. The voice belonged to Jim Gibson.

I flushed, but dug in. "Your education plan." I waved the leaflet and said, "Have you talked to teachers? How many years since you've been in a classroom?"

"Too long, I'm sure," he said. "Are you a teacher?"

"First grade at Washington Elementary."

"Jim, this is Lacey Corbett," Adella noted.

We shook hands, but before I could say anything, a man appeared and began pulling Gibson away.

"We'll have to continue this later," he said as he departed.

The following Monday afternoon, my class was involved in Show and Tell. A child had brought his white rat.

"Don't take it out of the cage," I cautioned, albeit a little too late. The lid was open, and the rat was loose. Some kids shrieked; others gave chase.

"Children, sit down," I hollered, but the noise level had reached hysteria. I joined the pursuit. The rat hid under a cabinet. I got down on my knees and peered underneath. The children clustered around. Beady pink eyes stared at me from the dark.

"Miss Corbett!" a child cried. "We have company."

I swiveled my head and looked up.

"Lose something?" Jim Gibson asked.

"A rat. It got loose. Got any ideas?"

He spotted a paper tube we'd been using in an art project and grabbed it. "This used to work on my gerbils," he said, joining me on the floor and sticking the tube under the cabinet. The rat saw the dark tube and ran into it. Jim quickly slid the tube out, covered both ends, and transported the rat to its cage.

"There's never a dull moment," I said.

"Do you mind if I stay awhile?" he asked.

"Not at all."

Jim stayed the rest of the school day, and then asked if he could take me to dinner. Over dinner we talked about education, and we pretty much agreed on everything. Maybe I had been hasty in my judgment.

At my door, he shook my hand and thanked me for a wonderful evening. I felt weak in the knees at his touch.

That evening was the first of several spent together, and we soon discovered we had much in common, beyond views on education. He was a really good listener. But I figured that came with the territory of politicking: He made everyone feel important. I was beginning to wish his attention was reserved just for me.

After our fourth dinner "meeting," I let slip that my dad was in the "other party."

"Precinct worker, committee person, all that," I told Jim.

"That's great. I like people who get involved. I'd like to meet him; maybe I can split his ticket."

I heard myself asking and Jim agreeing to come to Sunday dinner at my parents' house.

I okayed things with my mom and then worried all week. What had come over me? This would be a disaster.

But Sunday evening was totally amazing. Jim had my dad, the old veteran of smoke-filled rooms, eating out of his hand.

After dinner, Jim and I headed for the porch swing. "You may have done the impossible today," I said.

"What's that?" he asked.

"Won my dad's vote."

"Really?" He was quiet for a moment. "Well, that's not enough."

"What do you mean?"

"I have a bigger goal." He stopped the swing and turned toward me. His fingertips brushed a strand of my hair from my eyes and lingered on my cheek. "I want to win his daughter's heart."

And with that he leaned forward and kissed me. I didn't tell him then, because my lips were far too busy to talk, but he'd won *that* campaign weeks ago.[2]

From Two Lyrics

Let my voice ring out and over the earth,

Through all the grief and strife,

With a golden joy in a silver mirth

Thank God for Life!

Let my voice swell out through the great abyss

To the azure dome above,

With a chord of faith in the harp of bliss:

Thank God for Love!

Let my voice thrill out beneath and above,

The whole world through:

O my Love and Life, O my Life and Love,

Thank God for you!

JAMES THOMPSON

Did You Know? The 1956 film *High Society* was Grace Kelly's last before leaving movie roles for the role of wife to Prince Rainier of Monaco. To demonstrate she had no regrets about leaving Hollywood behind, Kelly wore her huge diamond engagement ring throughout the filming process.

Cook Up a Little Love

You can add some heat and spice to your marriage, both figuratively and literally, by preparing a meal with your spouse. You can discover a lot about a person by teaming up on a culinary endeavor. Childhood memories, food-related likes and dislikes, and tales of famous kitchen catastrophes—they all have a way of popping up in the kitchen. If one of you is a much better chef, this date will let you share the joy of teaching and learning. If you both fancy yourselves as "top chef masters," you can stir some good-natured competition into the mix.

Cost: This will depend on the type of meal you prepare, but even if you go all-out, a home-prepared gourmet meal will cost you less than half what you'd pay at a high-end restaurant.

Make the Date Deluxe: Take a cooking class together. This can be a lot of fun, and it's a great bonding experience. In fact, some corporations send employees to a cooking class to help them learn and appreciate the value of teamwork and cooperation. Another option is to invite friends over to share in the fruits of your labor. If you are the bold type, you could even ask your guests to rate various dishes.

Resources: Use a favorite family cookbook, or if you want to be ambitious, check out the websites for one of the current television cooking shows for recipes and meal ideas. Another twist on this date: commit to "winging it," creating an entire meal using only items currently in your pantry, refrigerator, and freezer.

The Original Love Story

GOD said, "It's not good for the Man to be alone;
I'll make him a helper, a companion."...

GOD put the Man into a deep sleep. As he slept he
removed one of his ribs and replaced it with flesh. God
then used the rib that he had taken from the Man to
make Woman and presented her to the Man.

The Man said,
"Finally! Bone of my bone,
flesh of my flesh!
Name her Woman
for she was made from Man."

Therefore, a man leaves his father and mother
and embraces his wife. They become one flesh.

GENESIS 2:18, 21–24

Greet one another with a kiss of love.

1 PETER 5:14, NRSV

I Love You

I love you for what you are, but I love you
yet more for what you are going to be.
I love you not so much for your realities
as for your ideals.
I pray for your desires that they may be great,
rather than for your satisfactions,
which may be so hazardously little.
You are going forward toward something great.
I am on the way with you,
and therefore I love you.

Carl Sandburg

Did You Know? Why do grooms customarily carry their brides across the threshold? Long ago in Scotland, it was believed that newlyweds' thresholds were cursed by witches. However, it was also believed that the groom could thwart the curse by carrying his bride across the doorsill and depositing her safely inside.

Made-for-TV Matches

In honor of Couple Appreciation Month (April), the website Funriper.com names its favorite television couples. Here is some of the latest list (from 2011), presented alphabetically. We've also added a few old favorites from years gone by. See if your favorite television twosome made the list.

Cliff and Clair Huxtable,
from *The Cosby Show*

Dan and Roseanne Conner,
from *Rosanne*

Dick and Laura Petrie
from *The Dick Van Dyke Show*

Eric and Tami Taylor,
from *Friday Night Lights*

Fox Mulder and Dana Scully,
from *The X-Files*

Homer and Marge Simpson,
from *The Simpsons*

Howard and Marion Cunningham,
from *Happy Days*

Jim and Pam Halpert,
from *The Office* (U.S. version)

Julius and Rochelle Rock,
from *Everybody Hates Chris*

Lucy and Ricky Ricardo,
from *I Love Lucy*

Matt Dillon and Miss Kitty,
from *Gunsmoke*

Mike and Carol Brady,
from *The Brady Bunch*

Ross and Rachel,
from *Friends*

Did You Know? The legend of the artist Vincent van Gogh and his ear is true, partially. The artist did sever his earlobe to impress a young woman named Rachel. He sent the lobe to Rachel, along with the message, "Guard this object carefully." Unimpressed, Rachel reported van Gogh to the local authorities.

Did You Know? The famous farmer couple depicted in the Grant Wood painting *American Gothic* were not a husband and wife. Nor were they father and daughter, or even farmers. The man was Wood's dentist, and the woman was Wood's sister.

BERRY SWEET
BREAKFAST PARFAITS
FOR TWO

1 cup low-fat cottage cheese
$1/2$ cup low-fat granola
1 cup mixed berries—strawberries, blueberries,
    raspberries, etc.
2 teaspoons chopped almonds

In two serving dishes, layer $1/4$ cup of cottage cheese, $1/8$ cup of granola, and $1/4$ cup of the mixed berries. Then repeat these layers in each dish. Top each parfait with 1 teaspoon of almonds and enjoy together!

The art of love...is largely the art of persistence.

ALBERT ELLIS

Love at First Sight

A BIBLICAL TALE, RETOLD BY VICKI J. KUYPER

It's an impulsive kiss. Tender, yet timid. Driven by passion, yet tempered with the fear of rejection. As Rachel pulls back from Jacob's unexpected embrace, Jacob slowly opens his eyes, drinking in every detail of the strikingly beautiful woman who stands before him. The one with the curl of auburn hair peeking out of her scarf, the glittering olive-green eyes and delicately curved fingers. The one who's made Jacob believe in love at first sight. The one he longs to call his bride.

Rachel's eyes meet Jacob's for just a moment, then dart self-consciously toward the ground. Jacob wants to say something, anything, to reassure Rachel that his intentions are honorable. But the moment he laid eyes on Laban's daughter, words fled like frightened sheep. Now all that remains are tears of thanks to the God who has led him here.

A group of shepherds gathered nearby watch the encounter with curiosity. Every day at this same time they come together to talk as they water their sheep. But today, just moments before, this stranger from Canaan arrived from the south. The traveler had inquired about the health of his relative, Laban, when suddenly the young man's attention turned to the western fields. There he saw a shepherdess herding her flock toward the well.

"That's Laban's daughter, Rachel," one of the shepherds began. But Jacob seemed caught up in a dream. He left the shepherd in midsentence and hurried to the young woman's side.

The band of men watched in amazement as Jacob pushed aside the large stone that covered the mouth of the well, the stone they had planned to move once all of the local shepherds arrived. It took at least five of them, working together, to shift the awkwardly heavy slab of rock each day. But this stranger, who in appearance certainly seemed to be a mere man, moved it as though it were made of reeds. Then came the stolen kiss.

Now that same stranger sits on the ground, his head in hands, weeping, as Rachel stands nearby. She seems pale, almost breathless as she tries to attend to watering her sheep. She pauses for a moment, gently placing her hand on the man's shoulder and whispers something in his ear. Perhaps the kiss was not stolen after all.

The local shepherds shake their heads, mutter a few words to each other under their breath, and then get back to work caring for their sheep. The next day when the shepherds gather at the well, Rachel never arrives. But the news already has. Laban has promised Rachel's hand in marriage to the smitten stranger. Since Jacob has no money to pay the customary bride price, he's agreed to work in Laban's fields for seven years.

As the years pass, Jacob tells his friends—the shepherds he first met at the well—over and over about the blessing God brought his way that day. How he traveled from Canaan to find a bride, a daughter from the family of his mother's brother, Laban. He repeats how his love story is so much like that of his father, Isaac, who also married a woman from Haran. For Isaac and Rebekah, just like for him and Rachel, it's a tale of love at first sight. But Jacob never shares the other side of the story. The real reason he left Canaan. How he deceived his father to steal his older brother's birthright. That part of his past remains a secret. That part of the past he tries to forget.

For seven years Jacob continues to tell his friends how working Laban's land is a small price to pay for a treasure like Rachel. "When you're in love," he always says with a grin, "years fly by like days."

At last, Jacob is counting down minutes instead of days, months, or years. The wedding feast has begun! Laban's home is filled with friends and relatives, music, food, and wine. Jacob's hearty laugh can be heard above the hubbub of song and celebration. Laban's sons gather around Jacob, offering blessing after blessing for a home filled with children, heirs to carry on the family name. As Jacob revels in his newfound family, he notices that Rachel's older sister, Leah, is no-where to be seen. Quiet and rather awkward, Leah has always been nervous around crowds.

She's probably sitting alone in a corner somewhere... Jacob's thoughts are interrupted by the hush of voices as the bride enters the room, escorted by her father. She's wrapped in red, her features hidden behind the intricately decorated wedding veil that covers her from head to toe. But Jacob can picture his bride as clearly as if the billow-ing veil were made of air. He can see the stray curl of red hair that re-fuses to be tamed dancing on her forehead. The warmth of her smile, so timid when she's with others, but always in full bloom whenever he's by her side. The willowy curve of her neck. The emerald fire that lights her eyes.

Laban puts the bride's hand into Jacob's. The father of the bride of-fers a blessing and then guides the couple into the room where they will spend their first night together. Not a single candle burns inside. Like another veil separating him from his bride, the darkness closes around Jacob as Laban shuts the door. With the noise of the feast still continuing down the hall, the room seems strangely quiet and still. Not a word passes between Jacob and his long-awaited bride. As Ja-cob's hands pull the veil aside in the dark, and his lips search the night for the one he loves, it seems words are unnecessary.

But as the morning light lifts the veil of night, plenty of words are on Jacob's tongue. Angry words. Tear-filled words. Words filled with venom and accusation. They begin the moment the groom awakens to find his bride already alert, her eyes downcast, ashamed to meet his. They are chestnut eyes, rimmed with dark lashes. It's Leah, not Rachel, who shares his bed.

Out in the courtyard, Laban greets Jacob's tirade with an air of indifference. "It's not the custom in our land to marry the younger daughter before the eldest is wed," Jacob's uncle says, his lips twisting into a smirk.

Jacob knows deceit when he sees it. The truth is, he knows it all too well. His own trickery is what made him flee Canaan in the first place. His own shame overshadows his anger. As the color rises in his cheeks, he becomes silent. But within himself a cry echoes loud and clear: *The deceiver has become the deceived.*

Laban breaks the silence. "I have an idea," Laban says, his calculated smile growing even wider. "Finish out your bridal week with my eldest daughter. Then you can marry Rachel. The bride price remains the same. Seven years."

Jacob looks up to see Rachel standing in the arch of the doorway. Her eyes are rimmed with tears. Almost hidden in her shadow stands Leah, her eyes on the ground, her hands hidden in the folds of her robe. Jacob stares at the two women, their lives bound together with the cords of love and deceit, passion and indifference.

"I'll work," Jacob replies. "I'll work for what's mine."[3]

God Keep You

God keep you, dearest, all this lonely night:
The winds are still,
The moon drops down behind the western hill;
God keep you safely, dearest, till the light.

God keep you then when slumber melts away,
And care and strife
Take up new arms to fret our waking life,
God keep you through the battle of the day.

God keep you. Nay, beloved soul, how vain,
How poor is prayer!
But I can but say again, and yet again,
God keep you every time and everywhere.

MADELINE BRIDGES

There is no remedy for love but to love more.

HENRY DAVID THOREAU

There is only one happiness in life, to love and be loved.

GEORGE SAND

Let us make God the beginning and end of our love, for he is the fountain from which all good things flow and into him alone they flow back.

RICHARD ROLLE OF HAMPOLE

Love isn't like a reservoir. You'll never drain it dry. It's much more like a natural spring. The longer and farther it flows, the stronger and deeper and clearer it becomes.

EDDIE CANTOR

The first duty of love is to listen.

PAUL TILLICH

Special Occasion Gift Idea

Does your sweetheart spend a lot of time in the car? If so, consider creating a custom playlist special to the two of you. Don't forget to include "your song." If you don't know how, ask one of your more tech-savvy friends to give you a hand. This is a one-of-a-kind gift that never fails to delight.

Kissing Trivia

Kissing releases the same neurotransmitters (chemical messengers in the brain) as those that are released when you engage in intense exercise such as running a marathon or skydiving. This causes your heart to beat faster and your breathing to become deep and irregular.

Wedding Trivia

The practice of giving or exchanging engagement rings began in 1477 when the Roman emperor, Maximilian I, gave Mary of Burgundy a diamond ring as an engagement present.

Wedding Trivia

According to English folklore, Saturday, the most popular American choice, is the unluckiest day to wed!

Wedding Trivia

The wedding veil dates back to ancient Rome, when it was flame-yellow, always worn over the face, and called a *flammeum*.

Kissing Trivia

The science of kissing is called *philematology*.

Song

You bound strong sandals on my feet,
You gave me bread and wine,
And sent me under sun and stars,
For all the world was mine.

Oh, take the sandals off my feet,
You know not what you do;
For all my world is in your arms,
My sun and stars are you.

<small>SARA TEASDALE</small>

Did You Know? In the movie *The Thomas Crown Affair*, the famous minute-long kiss scene between Steve McQueen and Faye Dunaway took more than eight hours to film, over the course of several days.

A REPORT FROM THE FRONT

Gary and Alexandra Grant had attended the same church for twenty years. Gary slept in on the odd Sunday, or went golfing with his buddies, but Alexandra rarely missed a service. So she was despondent one winter morning when a bad cold kept her in bed. Gary offered to stay home with her, so that he could care for her (and keep tabs on the first week of the NFL play-offs). Alexandra demanded that her husband go to church. The moment he returned, she demanded a full recap, which went like this:

Alexandra: "Was the service as good as ever this morning?"

Gary: "Yep. Good."

Alexandra: "What about the special music?"

Gary: "Good."

Alexandra: "I know attendance is low on cold days like this; how was the turnout?"

Gary: "Good."

Alexandra: "What was the sermon about?"

Gary: "The importance of good communication."

Love Booster
When you argue, focus on solving the problem at hand, not on "winning" the argument.

Out of the depths of my happy heart wells a great tide of love and prayer for this priceless treasure that is confided to my life-long keeping.

You cannot see its intangible waves as they flow toward you, darling, but in these lines you will hear, as if it were, the distant beating of its surf.

Forever yours,
Sam

FROM MARK TWAIN (SAMUEL LANGHORNE CLEMENS)
TO HIS FIANCÉE, OLIVIA LANGDON

The Drive-In Movie: A Blast from the Past

While perhaps not as popular as in their glory days, drive-in movies have been making a comeback in recent years, and at least one of these hidden treasures can be found in many cities. They boast huge screens, and many have updated sound systems that broadcast over your car stereo. Some drive-ins will show two or even three movies in a single night, so you get a lot of entertainment for your money. A night spent under the stars at the drive-in is so much more than just watching a movie—it's a fun, nostalgic, romantic experience you won't soon forget.

Cost: Most drive-in admissions are equal to or less than a couple of multiplex tickets, but remember to bring some extra cash for the snack bar. And, if you're extra budget conscious, bring your own snacks. You won't even have to hide them from ticket takers and ushers!

Make the Date Deluxe: Go online and search for a drive-in that sounds especially fun or is historically significant. If such a drive-in is far from home, make a road trip of it. Find a fun place to eat on the way.

Resources: The websites www.driveinmovie.com and www.driveintheater .com are both great sources for anything you need to know about drive-in theaters, from their history to up-to-date listings and descriptions of operating drive-ins in the United States.

Love Buster
Bring up your spouse's past mistakes. Never let them be buried.

What's in a Name?

What do you call that special someone in your life? If you'd like some inspiration to keep those little endearments coming, consider the choices below. Choose the fifty-two you like best and use a new one every week!

All Mine, Angel, Angel Baby, Angel Bunny, Angel Eyes, Angel Face, Angel-on-Earth, Babe, Babes, Babushka, Baby, Baby Angel, Baby Bear, Baby Boo, Baby Cakes, Baby Doll, Baby Doodle, Baby Face, Baby Girl, Baby Love, Babycheeks, Babylicious, Bad Kitty, Beautiful, Big Daddy, Big Dawg, Big Diesel, Big Guy, Big Kitty, Blue Eyes, Bombshell, Boo, Boo Bear, Boo-Boo, Boogie Bear, Braveheart, Bright Eyes, Brown Sugar, Bubba, Bubbles, Bunny, Buttercup, Butterfly, Butterscotch, Canoodle, Captain, Care Bear, Cheesecake, Cherry Pie, Chickadee, Chocolate, Chocolate Bunny, Chocolate Drop, Cookie, Cool Breeze, Cowboy, Cuddle Bear, Cuddle Bug, Cuddle Bunny, Cuddle Cakes, Cuddles, Cupcake, Cupid, Cuppy Cake, Cutie, Cutie Pie, Cutiehead, Darling, Darlington, Dear, Dearest, Dearest One, Dearheart, Deep Waters, Dimples, Doctor Love, Doctor Feelgood, Doll Face, Doodle Bug, Dove, Dreamlover, Firecracker, Firework, Firefly, Fluffy, Goose, Gorgeous, Gumdrop, Gummie Bear, Handsome, Hon, Honey, Honey Bear, Honey Bee, Honey Bunch, Honey Bunny, Honey Buns, Honey Lamb, Honey Lips, Honey Love, Honey Muffin, Honey Pie, Honey Plum, Hot Babe, Hot Honey, Hot Mama, Hot Stuff, Hotcakes, Hottie, Hottie-Katottie, Hubby Wubby,

Ironman, King of Kiss, Kit Kat, Kitten, Lady Bug, Lemon Drop, Lieutenant Love, Little Kinky, Little Mama, Little Monkey, Little Muppet, Lollipop, Love, Love Angel, Love Bear, Love Bug, Love Heart, Love Machine, Love Monkey, Love Muffin, Love Nugget, Love Sponge, Loveable, Love-a-lump, Lovebird, Lover, Lover Boy, Lover Bunny, Lover Girl, Lovey Dovey, Lovie, Luvs, Luvin' Spoonful, Man-Child, Merlin, Mi Amor, Mistress, Monkey, Muffin, Munchkin, My Angel, My Beloved, My Buttercup, My Heart, My King, My Lion, My Love, My Lovely, My Queen, Papa Bear, Papi, Passion Flower, Passion Fruit, Petal, Pooh Bear, Pookie, Pookie Bear, Precious, Precious Angel, Precious Princess, Pretty Lady, Prince, Prince Charming, Princess, Princess Passion, Puddin', Pumpkin, Punkin', Puppy, Pussycat, Queen of Kiss, Red Rose, Scrumptious, Sexy Thang, Smoochie Poo, Snickerdoodle, Snookie, Snookums, Snow Bunny, Snow Pea, Snowflake, Snuggle Bear, Snuggle Bug, Snuggle Bunny, Snuggle Pooh, Snuggles, Sparky Star, Starfish, Starshine, Stud Muffin, Sugar, Sugar Babe, Sugar Bear, Sugar Biscuit, Sugar Britches, Sugar Buns, Sugar Cookie, Sugar Daddy, Sugar Lips, Sugar Mama, Sugar Muffin, Sugar Pie, Sugar Pumpkin, Sugarplum, Sunshine, Superman, Sweet, Sweet Baby, Sweet Cheeks, Sweet Kitten, Sweet Lover, Sweet Pea, Sweet Peach, Sweet Stuff, Sweet Tart, Sweetheart, Sweetie, Sweetie Pie, Sweetness, Sweets, Sweetums, Sweety Cakes, Tadwinks, Teddy, Teddy Bear, Temptress, Tiger, Tigress, Tomcat, Tootsie Roll, Tulip, Tweetums, Twinkie, Twinkle Toes, Waffles, Wiggles, Wild Thing, Woobie, Wookie, Wookums, Wuggle Bear, Wuggles, Yummy Bear

BREAKFAST-IN-BED BANANA-NUT PROTEIN PANCAKES

1 banana
$1/4$ cup rolled oats
2 tablespoons low-fat cottage cheese
2 egg whites
$1/2$ tablespoon vanilla extract

Blend all ingredients until batter is smooth. If desired, stir in 2 teaspoons of chopped walnuts or pecans. In a skillet or on a griddle coated with nonstick cooking spray, cook pancakes over medium heat about three minutes on each side. If desired, drizzle with maple syrup and top with slices of banana. Yield: 2 medium pancakes. Double or triple if you and your sweetie are extra hungry.

We Thank You, Lord

Lord, behold our family here assembled.
We thank you for this place in which we dwell,
for the love that unites us,
for the peace accorded us this day...
for the health, the work, the food and the
bright skies that make our lives delightful;
for our friends in all parts of the earth.

　Amen.

ROBERT LOUIS STEVENSON

Love Booster
Ask questions that show you are genuinely interested in
what your spouse is saying.

At the touch of love, everyone becomes a poet.

PLATO

Love should run out to meet love with open arms.

WILLIAM SHAKESPEARE

*Gravitation cannot be held responsible
for people falling in love.*

ALBERT EINSTEIN

*A happy marriage is a long conversation
which always seems too short.*

ANDRÉ MAUROIS

Love is an act of endless forgiveness,
a tender look which becomes a habit.

PETER USTINOV

PERFECT PAIR
ANNIE OAKLEY
AND FRANK BUTLER

At age fifteen, Annie Oakley defeated a professional marksman named Frank Butler in a shooting competition. But instead of resenting the young sharpshooter's victory, Butler fell in love with her. A year later, the duo married and Butler became his five-foot-tall wife's assistant on the traveling Buffalo Bill's Wild West Show. Butler trusted his wife's skill so much that their act included Annie's shooting a dime out of her husband's hand and a cigarette from his mouth. Annie, who learned to shoot at age eight, could also hit a playing card tossed into the air by Butler, at a distance of ninety feet.

(Incidentally, in her later years, Annie served as a shooting instructor for the U.S. military during World War I.)

More Than a Heart Can Hold

A BIBLICAL TALE, RETOLD BY VICKI J. KUYPER

How can one heart hold so many tears? Ruth's mind turns to question the "how" instead of the "why" of this new heartbreak. It's easier that way. She's already struggled with the "why" of not being able to conceive a child. The "why" of her brother-in-law's sudden death. The "why" of the loss of Mahlon, the man she loved, her husband and friend. Now, she finds herself standing at a crossroad, physically and emotionally.

A warm afternoon wind whips the cloth of the black mourning clothes across the face of her widowed mother-in-law, but not before Ruth sees that Naomi's eyes are as filled with tears as are her own. They have all lost so much. Three women in black—Ruth, Naomi, and Orpah, Naomi's other daughter-in-law. All of them widows. All of them left without heirs, without provision for their needs, without hope.

Ruth knows that's why Naomi is asking her daughters-in-law to return home to their own families. Naomi hopes they may still have a chance to find another husband, to secure a different future for themselves. Naomi's accepted that her future has but one path. She will return to Bethlehem, the land she and her husband left years before when the famine forced them south to Moab. There she'll call on the generosity of her relatives. Perhaps their faith, and their pity, will move them to care for a poor widow. But three widows?

Ruth knows Naomi loves her and Orpah as deeply as if they'd been her daughters by birth. She knows it's that love that compels Naomi to say good-bye, even though it means another loss, another heartbreak.

But still Ruth can't let go. She holds on to Naomi's frail shoulders with the tender care of a child rescuing a bird that's fallen from its nest. Naomi tries to pull away, but Ruth grabs the cloth of her mother-in-law's shawl and falls to her knees in the dirt.

"Look!" Naomi pleads with Ruth, pointing toward Orpah who is stumbling slowly back toward town, the young woman's shoulders racked with sobs. "Your sister-in-law is going back to her people and her gods. Go back with her."

"Don't urge me to leave you or to turn back from you!" Ruth pleads. "Where you go I will go, and where you stay I will stay. Your people will be my people and your God my God."

Naomi takes Ruth's hand in her own and pulls it toward her heart. Ruth rises to look her beloved mother-in-law in the eye.

"Then let us go," Naomi says softly. Ruth can't tell whether it's sorrow or gratitude she hears beneath her words.

Their walk to Judah is long, dusty, and dry. It's the most distant, most desolate, journey Ruth has ever taken. Some days she wonders if her mother-in-law will even survive the trip. But as their supply of food draws near an end, Naomi begins to recognize long-forgotten landmarks. She becomes more animated as she tells Ruth stories of her childhood and about the early days of her marriage to Elimelech. Suddenly, she grows quiet.

"Naomi," Ruth tries to reassure her, "it will be alright. We're almost there."

"Don't call me Naomi," her mother-in-law says with a cold edge to her voice. "That means 'pleasant.' From now call me Mara, which means 'bitter.' For I left this land full and now I'm returning empty."

Though Naomi seems to warm a bit at the welcome her relatives extend as she and Ruth settle into town, Ruth worries about the bitter seed that seems to have taken root in her mother-in-law's heart.

Determined to provide for Naomi in any way she can, Ruth rises early the next day to glean in a nearby barley field. It's the work of the poor, picking up grain that paid harvest workers miss. But Ruth's love for Naomi is stronger than her pride.

Ruth's back begins to ache as the sun rises high in the sky. She balances a small basket of barley on her hip as she makes her way up and down the rows of grain. Suddenly Ruth notices she's alone in the field. The other harvesters have made their way toward the shade of a leafy tree where the field's foreman is talking with a well-dressed man.

Even from where she stands, Ruth can hear the deep rumble of the man's voice greeting the harvesters. "The Lord be with you!" he says.

"The Lord bless you!" one after another replies.

Ruth lowers her eyes and gets back to work. Naomi's depending on her. She can't stop for small talk.

"Welcome!" a man's voice startles Ruth, almost sending a shower of barley from her basket back onto the ground. She looks up into the eyes of the well-dressed man, now close to her side. Though the man's hair is sprinkled with gray, his broad shoulders show the strength of someone who's not a stranger to physical labor. But the man's face doesn't show the deep lines of those who spend their lives working under the hot sun. Instead, it's smooth and lightly bronzed, with finely cut features offset by a slightly crooked smile.

"I'm so glad you've come to work in my fields," he says softly. "I hope you'll continue working here as long as you'd like. I've told the men to leave you alone, but do stay close to the other women. And feel free to drink from the water jars whenever you're thirsty."

Ruth drops to her knees in a sign of respect, placing her face low to the ground. "Sir, I'm a foreigner here. Why have I found such kind favor in your eyes?"

"Please call me Boaz," the man replies. He bends down to help Ruth to her feet and then continues, "I've heard of what you've done for my relative Naomi. How you left your father and your mother and your home and came to live with people you've never met. May the Lord repay you for what you've done. May you be richly rewarded by the Lord, the God of Israel, under whose wings you've come to take refuge.

"Are you hungry?" he asks Ruth, who's at a loss for what to say. She mumbles out a soft, "Yes," to which Boaz replies, "Please join us for some food."

As Ruth seats herself in the shade with the other women, Boaz walks over to where the men are resting. Under his breath, he tells his foreman, "Let this woman gather wherever she wants. Drop a few stalks of barley along the way for her to glean with the heads of grain. Don't embarrass her. Just be generous. Just as God has been to us."

Boaz returns to Ruth with bread and some roasted grain. Then with a smile and a nod of his head, Boaz turns and walks back through the fields toward the threshing floor. The rest of the afternoon passes quickly, as Ruth's hands seem to keep pace with the thoughts tumbling through her mind.

I can't wait to show Naomi all of the grain I've gathered! I must have gleaned over half a bushel already—on my first day! Boaz seems like such a kind man...and a handsome man. His smile seemed to say more to me than his words... But what am I thinking? Of course, he's just helping me to help Naomi. Isn't he? I haven't felt this way since my parents arranged my marriage to Mahlon... Stop daydreaming, you foolish woman! Don't let your emotions run away with you...

But that night Naomi's emotions seem as filled with girlish daydreams as Ruth's. "The Lord hasn't forgotten us!" Naomi says with a joyful clap of her wrinkled hands. "He's led you straight to one of our kinsmen-redeemers! Boaz is one of my closest relatives. Therefore by law he has the choice of purchasing your husband's property and marrying you. Now here's what you need to do."

Weeks pass as Ruth and Naomi wait for just the right time to put Naomi's plan into action. One evening when Ruth returns from working in the fields, Naomi greets her at the door with a wide smile. It's a smile Ruth's grown to look forward to over the last few weeks, a smile that shows God is gleaning the bitterness from Naomi's heart.

"Tonight Boaz will be winnowing barley on the harvesting floor," Naomi says with delight. "Go get washed up! Use that last bit of perfume. Put on your best clothes. The Lord will be with you as you go."

The plan is finally in motion.

Boaz is startled awake from a sound sleep. He lifts his head up from his makeshift bed beside a pile of grain. Every year at winnowing time this is his bedroom, his outer robe thrown on the threshing floor. His feet are cold. He must have kicked the robe off during the night. His eyes strain to find anything out of place in the darkness. Something moves at his feet.

"Who's there? Who is it?" Boaz cries out in the darkness.

"Don't be afraid!" Ruth reassures Boaz. "It's your servant, Ruth. Please, sir, spread the corner of your garment over me. You're my kinsman-redeemer."

For a moment, there's silence. Then, Boaz says softly, "The Lord bless you.... Not only have you honored your mother-in-law by loving her as faithfully as any true daughter ever could, but now you've honored me with your request! Instead of running after younger relatives, you've chosen to come to me. I'll cover you with the garment of my protection and provision. And I'll gladly take you as my wife so that your husband's name won't be forgotten or erased from our family.

The barley is ripening. Every breeze sets the grain dancing in the fields. Soon, the harvesters will return to their work under the hot sun. But Ruth's no longer in the fields. Instead, she watches Naomi lift her new grandson into her arms, nuzzling the soft chestnut fuzz on his head close to her cheek. Ruth's eyes fill with tears. But this time they overflow from a heart filled with joy, instead of sorrow.

As a neighbor woman walks by she shouts to Naomi, "Your daughter-in-law's love is better than seven sons!"

"It's true," Naomi replies, looking Ruth in the eyes. "I returned to this land empty and now my life is once again full. How the Lord has blessed me through you!"

How can one heart hold so much love? Ruth looks at the joy on Naomi's face and then takes a quick look back over the last few years. Love lost and then found again. Naomi, Boaz, and now Obed, a son. This land and this faith that at first felt so foreign, now feel like the only home Ruth's ever longed for.

"The Lord is with me!" she whispers, lifting her eyes to the azure skies. "And Lord, I am with You. Forever Yours."[3]

Love Buster

Multitask when your spouse is talking. Check your e-mails, read the paper, keep one eye on the television.

"LOVE APPLE" AND BASIL SOUP

1 tablespoon canola oil

1 ½ cups diced red onion

3 tablespoons minced fresh garlic

4 cups roughly chopped love apples (i.e., fresh tomatoes)

28 ounces vegetable broth

½ cup tomato paste

3 tablespoons chopped basil

Salt to taste

White or black pepper to taste

Juice of half a lemon

Heat canola oil in a large pot for 2 minutes on medium heat. Sauté onions in the oil for about 5 minutes (avoid browning). Mix in garlic. Add love apples, broth, and tomato paste. Bring to a boil, then reduce to simmer for 20 minutes, or until love apples are soft. Remove from heat and add basil. Blend in food processor or blender for 2 minutes, or until mixture is smooth. Season with salt, pepper, and lemon juice.

Note: Tomatoes were once called love apples because they were believed to be an aphrodisiac.

Epitaph

This poem was written for the tomb of Olivia Langdon Clemens, wife of Mark Twain.

Warm summer sun,

shine kindly here.

Warm southern wind,

blow softly here.

Green sod above,

lie light, lie light.

Good night, dear heart,

Good night, good night.

My Heart Is at Rest

When the voices of children

Are heard on the green

And laughing is heard on the hill,

My heart is at rest within my breast

And everything else is still.

WILLIAM BLAKE

Love's Wings

There is nothing holier in this life of ours than the first

consciousness of love—

The first fluttering of its silken wings—

The first rising sound and breath of that wind,

Which is so soon to sweep through the soul,

To purify or to destroy.

HENRY WADSWORTH LONGFELLOW

Did You Know? In the insect kingdom, the male cicada plays a love song for potential mates using a pair of ribbed membranes on his abdomen. Some varieties of cicadas sing their love song at 120 decibels, which is the pain threshold for the human ear.

Two are better than one, because they have a good reward
for their toil. For if they fall, one will lift up the other; but woe
to one who is alone and falls and does not have another to help.
Again, if two lie together, they keep warm; but how can one
keep warm alone? And though one might prevail against
another, two will withstand one.

A threefold cord is not quickly broken.

ECCLESIASTES 4:9–12, NRSV

Love covers over all wrongs.

PROVERBS 10:12, NIV

May the Lord make your love increase
and overflow for each other and for everyone else.

1 THESSALONIANS 3:12, NIV

St. Valentine's Day

Give her a hug this morning,

Give her the old-time kiss—

From the calendar's first to final,

There's only one day like this.

Rumple her hair a little,

In the old-time tender way,

Show her you haven't forgotten...This is

St. Valentine's Day.

Never take love for granted,

Don't be afraid to speak—

While you are pouring his coffee,

Fondle his whiskered cheek.

And over his shoulder bending,

"I love you," be sure to say.

Now is the time to do it...

This is St. Valentine's Day.

If lovers at times seem foolish,

As cynics will agree,

Then this is the very morning

When foolish it's wise to be.

We all need a lot more loving,

And more of true love's display,

So, let's be a little silly...

This is St. Valentine's Day.

Edgar A. Guest

A Song of Love

Do you and your sweetie have a love tune that you claim as "our song"? Recently, the website About.com named its top 100 love songs. Did your song make the list?

100. "Head Over Heels" by Tears for Fears

99. "Ain't No Other Man" by Christina Aguilera

98. "Escape (The Piña Colada Song)" by Rupert Holmes

97. "Baby Baby" by Amy Grant

96. "You Needed Me" by Anne Murray

95. "Evergreen" by Barbra Streisand

94. "Brand New Key" by Melanie

93. "Truly, Madly, Deeply" by Savage Garden

92. "Still the One" by Orleans

91. "The Best" by Tina Turner

90. "All My Life" by K-Ci and JoJo

89. "Stumblin' In" by Suzi Quatro and Chris Norman

88. "Up Where We Belong" by Joe Cocker and Jennifer Warnes

87. "My Love" by Justin Timberlake, featuring T.I.

86. "Save the Best for Last" by Vanessa Williams

85. "Rosanna" by Toto

84. "I Love Your Smile" by Shanice

83. "This Guy's in Love with You" by Herb Alpert

82. "Baby, I Love Your Way" by Peter Frampton

81. "Be Without You" by Mary J. Blige

80. "(Everything I Do) I Do It for You" by Bryan Adams

79. "Lovesong" by The Cure

78. "Love Will Keep Us Together" by Captain and Tennille

77. "When I Think of You" by Janet Jackson

76. "Endless Love" by Diana Ross and Lionel Richie

75. "I Think I Love You" by The Partridge Family

74. "Just What I Needed" by The Cars

73. "You're the First, My Last, My Everything" by Barry White

72. "I'll Make Love to You" by Boyz II Men

71. "Betcha by Golly, Wow" by The Stylistics

70. "Never Ending Song of Love" by Delaney & Bonnie and Friends

69. "Leather and Lace" by Stevie Nicks and Don Henley

68. "Your Body Is a Wonderland" by John Mayer

67. "Sweet Love" by Anita Baker

66. "If" by Bread

65. "Tie a Yellow Ribbon 'Round the Ole Oak Tree" by Dawn, featuring Tony Orlando

64. "Silly Love Songs" by Wings

63. "Longer" by Dan Fogelberg

62. "Never Tear Us Apart" by INXS

61. "Fields of Gold" by Sting

60. "Help Me" by Joni Mitchell

59. "Love Me Tender" by Elvis Presley

58. "My Heart Will Go On" by Celine Dion

57. "Jack & Diane" by John Cougar (Mellencamp)

56. "Here and Now" by Luther Vandross

55. "Ring of Fire" by Johnny Cash

54. "You Are the Sunshine of My Life" by Stevie Wonder

53. "A Whole New World" by Peabo Bryson and Regina Belle

52. "Nobody's Supposed to Be Here" by Deborah Cox

51. "Iris" by Goo Goo Dolls

50. "I'll Stand by You" by The Pretenders

49. "Maggie May" by Rod Stewart

48. "Time and Tide" by Basia

47. "Happy Together" by The Turtles

46. "(Just Like) Starting Over" by John Lennon

45. "You Send Me" by Sam Cooke

26. "Let's Get It On" by Marvin Gaye

25. "I Will Always Love You" by Whitney Houston

24. "When a Man Loves a Woman" by Percy Sledge

23. "My Guy" by Mary Wells

22. "Wonderwall" by Oasis

21. "(They Long to Be) Close to You" by The Carpenters

20. "Time After Time" by Cyndi Lauper

19. "The Closer I Get to You" by Roberta Flack and Donny Hathaway

18. "Higher and Higher" by Jackie Wilson

17. "Ain't No Mountain High Enough" by Marvin Gaye and Tammi Terrell

16. "I Got You Babe" by Sonny & Cher

15. "Solid" by Ashford & Simpson

14. "The Letter" by The Box Tops

13. "Hey There Delilah" by The Plain White T's

12. "Get Here" by Oleta Adams

11. "Tonight I Celebrate My Love" by Peabo Bryson and Roberta Flack

10. "Unchained Melody" by The Righteous Brothers

9. "I Melt with You" by Modern English

8. "Wonderful Tonight" by Eric Clapton

7. "And I Love Her" by The Beatles

6. "Chasing Cars" by Snow Patrol

5. "Just the Way You Are" by Billy Joel

4. "The First Time Ever I Saw Your Face" by Roberta Flack

3. "Maybe I'm Amazed" by Paul McCartney

2. "Your Song" by Elton John

1. "Something" by The Beatles

Love Booster
Admit mistakes and shortcomings—with humility and grace.

Did You Know? On May 7, 1990, pro baseball outfielder Chad Curtis married his fiancée, Candace, at a courthouse in Davenport, Iowa. Instead of a tux, Curtis sported his Quad Cities Angels uniform. Curtis's nuptial attire wasn't an attempt at humor. The ceremony took place at 1:30 p.m., just a half hour before the new groom took the field for an afternoon game.

Did You Know? To test the theory that a million monkeys with a million typewriters could produce a Shakespearean love sonnet, British researchers gave six short-tailed monkeys a computer, then sat back to observe the reaction. Some monkeys did hit a few keystrokes, mostly long strings of S's. But most of them used their computer as a toilet or beat it with rocks.

Did You Know? The wedding band that President Abraham Lincoln gave Mary Todd Lincoln was engraved with these words: "Love is eternal."

1894

See how it works out: it is agreed that we shall be great friends, but if you leave France in a year it would be an altogether too Platonic friendship, that of two creatures who would never see each other again. Wouldn't it be better for you to stay with me? I know that this question angers you, and that you don't want to speak of it again— and then, too, I feel so thoroughly unworthy of you from every point of view.

FROM PIERRE CURIE TO MARIA SKLODOVSKA (CURIE)

Wanna "Play" Around?

To add a little dramatic flair to your dating life, take your sweetie to a play or musical production. You can attend a big-budget production at a local performing-arts center, or you may want to check out the local talent of a community-theater group, attend a high-school or college production, or visit a small theater that showcases the works of local playwrights. Whatever your choice, you're sure to enjoy the mystery, make-believe, and magic of the stage.

Cost: The stage offers something for almost any budget. If you want great seats at a local performance of a big-time Broadway show, you could end up paying a hundred dollars or more for a pair of seats. Local community-theater performances will set you back eight or ten bucks a ticket. On the budget end of the spectrum, a performance of a musical at your local high school will cost only ten bucks or so for a pair of tickets. (And the refreshments at these productions are often inexpensive—and homemade!)

Make the Date Deluxe: If going to a play awakens the inner thespian in you both, consider joining a local theater group together or trying out for small parts in a play, such as a "Theater in the Park" production.

Resources: For a comprehensive listing of plays, both modern and classic, as well as their descriptions, go to drama.eserver.org. For online searches, try keywords such as *performing arts center, drama, theater, community theater,* and *Shakespeare in the park*. And, of course, discovering which musicals, dramas, and comedies are happening at your local schools is as easy as a phone call or a visit to a school website.

Are your hearts tender and compassionate?
Then make me truly happy by agreeing
wholeheartedly with each other, loving
one another, and working together.

PHILIPPIANS 2:1–2, NLT

These three remain: faith, hope and love.
But the greatest of these is love.

1 CORINTHIANS 13:13, NIV

Above all, maintain constant love for one another,
for love covers a multitude of sins.

1 PETER 4:8, NRSV

CONVERSATION STARTERS FOR COUPLES

Sometimes, the most meaningful and revealing conversations can start with a simple question. Here are just a few to get you started...

Who was your childhood hero—and is this person still a hero to you? Why? Or why not?

What one thing could I start doing that would make you a happier person?

What is your life's biggest regret—and how could I help to ease it?

What's the best book you've read this past year—and what did you like about it?

If you could visit any place in the world (and money was no factor), where would you go? Why?

What would you say is your number-one life goal right now?

Who was the best teacher you ever had—and why?

If you could personally ask Jesus one question, what would it be?

What is the biggest risk you've ever taken?

What is your earliest childhood memory?

If you had a theme song, what would it be?

In a movie of your life story, who would star in the role of *you*?

If you could eat only one food item for the rest of your life, what would it be?

What was your first impression of me?

What five words best describe our relationship as a couple?

What makes our marriage unique from other marriages?

How am I different from the man (or woman) of your teenage dreams? How am I similar?

FLOWER POWER?

A gentleman named Sam visited his pastor for some marital advice. "I really blew it, padre," Sam confessed. "Last Friday was the twenty-eighth anniversary for me and the missus, and I completely forgot about it. First time that's ever happened—and I swore it never would."

"Well, I know your wife," the pastor said, "and I think she'll forgive you. But you really should get her something nice—as both an anniversary gift and a symbol of your remorse."

Sam nodded. "Good idea. But do you have any suggestions on what to get her?"

The pastor pondered the question for several moments. "Personally," he said, "I've always been fond of the philosophy 'Say it with flowers.'"

Sam popped to his feet. "Great suggestion, padre. I think you just saved my bacon!"

The next day, Sam trudged back into the pastor's study, his chin drooping to his chest.

"Sam," the pastor said, "you look crestfallen. Didn't things go well at home?"

"No sir, they didn't. And I don't understand. After my visit with you, I picked up a rose on the way home and gave it to the missus the minute I got to the house."

The pastor shook his head. "Sam...just a single rose, after twenty-eight years of marriage? And after forgetting your anniversary in the first place? That's not what I'd call saying it with flowers."

Sam shrugged. "Well, I've always been a man of few words."

Young and in Love

Young and in love—how magical the phrase!
How magical the fact! Who has not yearned
Over young lovers when to their amaze
they fall in love, and find their love returned,
And the lights brighten, and their eyes are clear
to see God's image in their common clay.
Is it the music of the spheres they hear?
Is it the prelude to that noble play
to the drama of Joined Lives?

ALICE DUER MILLER, *The White Cliffs*

Did You Know? Before a "hot date," women of ancient Rome attempted to make their skin soft and sweet smelling by bathing in tubs filled with donkey milk mixed with a bit of swan's fat.

*Sexiness wears thin after a while and
beauty fades, but to be married to a man
who makes you laugh every day,
ah, now that's a real treat.*

JOANNE WOODWARD

*To get the full value of joy, you must
have someone to divide it with.*

MARK TWAIN

Look for a sweet person. Forget rich.

ESTÉE LAUDER

To love at all is to be vulnerable.

C. S. LEWIS

Love is like a friendship caught on fire.

BRUCE LEE

A Prayer of Hope for Two

Dear Loving God,

Help us to remember, when we begin to lose hope,
that all the darkness in the world
is just a speck in Your light,
a light that fills the universe.
When pain and confusion invade our lives,
let us not rely on our own resources.
Instead, lead us to seek answers on our knees.
Lord, show us Your way. Lord, lead us to Your destination.
We thank You for being our beacon of hope,
a beacon we can always see, if we will only look.

Amen.

MINTY FRESH
LOVE NECTAR

4 mint sprigs

1 teaspoon finely grated fresh ginger

4 ounces chilled pear nectar

4 ounces chilled sparkling white grape juice
    or ginger ale

Additional mint sprigs for garnish, if desired

Combine 2 mint sprigs and $\frac{1}{2}$ teaspoon ginger in each of two chilled glasses and mash well. Fill glasses with ice. Add half of nectar and grape juice or ginger ale to each glass. Garnish with mint sprigs, if desired, and serve immediately.

If Loving Means I'm Wrong, I Don't Wanna Be Right

By Jedd Hafer

As the youngest of four brothers, I took careful note as each of my siblings took the plunge into Lake Matrimony. Marriage seemed to agree with each of them. They dressed better, they looked happier, they bathed more regularly, and I kept getting free clothes—every time one of the wives found an article of clothing she despised.

Then, one day, it happened to me. I experienced the thrill my brothers had discovered years earlier. That fateful day when a special someone appears on your doorstep and you look through the peephole and proclaim, "Eureka! Behold the most wondrous person to grace my front porch since the pizza-delivery guy!"

Soon, wedding bells tinkled, overjoyed relatives almost tinkled, and I joined my brothers in the ranks of the married. Years have passed since that magical day, but I'm happy to say that my wife, Lindsey, is still the pure joy of my life. (I'm especially happy to say that if Lindsey is standing nearby at the time.)

Like my brothers, I now dress better, chew with my mouth closed, and buy breakfast cereal based on fiber content, not which toy is inside the box. Marriage brings changes, but I can honestly say that 99 percent of them are for the better.

In fact, I have discovered only one major drawback: As soon as you accept the fact that you are someone's husband, you must also accept the fact that you are suddenly—and without warning—incompetent at basically everything. And now you have someone to point out your incompetence every day for the rest of your life.

My first clue as to this new life station blew in on the winds of the wedding ceremony. As was the case with my brothers, I wasn't consulted about many details. My main job was to show up at the church on time and remember to wear socks. As a human groom, I had about as much responsibility as the little plastic groom atop our wedding cake.

In fact, someday soon I believe that plastic groom will disappear from all wedding cakes. The plastic bride will stand there holding hands with *her mom*. And, if technology allows, these two figurines will be able to talk with the press of a button, uttering true-life wedding-day sentiments such as, "Boo-hoo-hoo! We should have opted for the teal napkins! Boo-hoo-hoo!"

Why this groomian insignificance? It's simple. Grooms are kept in the background on the wedding day because brides know they will mess up everything if they try to get involved.

Of course, this tactic won't work for the rest of the marriage. Understand that the man is no more competent than he was on the wedding day; it's just that now he can't stand there in the frosting, trying to keep a low profile. Now he has to face the blame.

That's the main lesson I've learned since my wedding day. People used to ask me for advice and guidance on a variety of topics, from lawn care to dog-obedience training. But since getting married, I have discovered that I don't even know how to dress, groom, bathe, or feed myself properly. Also, I once believed I knew how to drive a car. Ha! It turns out that I don't know "the first thing" about piloting an automobile. That is why I need an expert driving instructor beside me at all times, critiquing my every turn, yield, and lane change. Oh, well, at least she's a strikingly beautiful driving instructor.

I guess it all comes down to the concept of blame. Before I was married, problems occurred in the world, and I felt no sense of direct responsibility about them. But after getting married, I have learned that I am eminently capable of messing up things that I don't even know about. Moreover, I can get into serious trouble for things I don't say—but look like I might be thinking.

If you're having a hard time grasping this concept, you are, most likely, a married man and therefore you're not very smart. So, to make things easier to understand, here is just one real-life example of just how wrong and incompetent a married guy can be, without even trying.

Recently, my wife flew out of state to visit her family. I missed her very much because she is the light of my life. (And I didn't write that just to earn brownie points by proclaiming my love forever in print, in a book that will be read by thousands of people.)

Upon Lindsey's return from the trip, I drove my car (carefully, adhering to all traffic regulations) to the airport to pick her up. I found a spot in short-term parking and walked to the terminal to meet my beloved bride. After a warm but tasteful embrace, we headed back to the short-term lot. As I veered toward our car, which I had parked just a few minutes previously, Lindsey said, "You're going the wrong way. This isn't where the car is parked."

At this point, we must review two key facts:

1. I, and I alone, parked the car.
2. While I was parking the car, Lindsey was thirty thousand feet in the air, asleep.

Are you following this? She couldn't have known I was wrong. She could only assume I was wrong. But in her mind, there was no assuming involved. She knew I was wrong, because I was the guy, and that's what guys do. We find ways to be wrong about stuff.

At this point, I guess I should add, as a minor footnote to this story, that, uh...

I was wrong about where the car was parked.

Yep, it took me thirty-five minutes to find that stupid car. And, as strange as it feels to admit it now, I found myself searching in lots that I knew were the wrong ones. I felt being magnetically pulled to one wrong lot after another. I felt my IQ dropping like a bad tech stock, and there was nothing I could do to stop it. I began to envy that little plastic groom.

So, yes, my life is frustrating sometimes, but I wouldn't trade it for anything. Considering how magical my wife makes my life, I would never want to be a plastic groom—even if he does get to stand up to his ankles in delicious frosting and avoid ever taking blame for anything. You see, married life is way sweeter than cake frosting.

Besides, I know I wouldn't get blamed for so many things if I'd be more open to correction from my wise spouse.

One final note is in order here: Lindsey made me write the previous sentence, but she was also the one who actually found our car at the airport, so there you go...[4]

Love Buster

Give weak, conditional apologies, like, "If I said something to hurt your feelings..."

Special Occasion Gift Idea

You might be surprised how amazing a handmade gift can be. Bake a cake, write a poem or a story or a song, knit a scarf, bake heart-shaped iced cookies. Create a special meal with all your sweetheart's favorites.

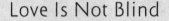

Love Is Not Blind

*Passion may be blind; but to say that love is,
is a libel and a lie. Nothing is more sharp-sighted
or sensitive than true love, in discerning, as by
an instinct, the feelings of another.*

WILLIAM HENRY DAVIS

On Lemonade and Love

AUTHOR UNKNOWN

Driving down a deserted Indiana road, I saw a "Fresh Lemonade" sign, so I pulled over. I had expected a filling station or small store, but to my surprise, it was a house. An old man sat on the porch. I got out of my car. Nobody else was around. He poured me some lemonade and offered me a seat. It was so peaceful—nothing but cornfields, sky, and sun in view.

We talked about the weather and my trip. He asked if I had family. I explained that I had just gotten married and hoped to have children someday. He seemed pleased that family still mattered to some folks.

Then he told me his story. I share it because it is one I cannot forget.

"There's something special about families. A wife, children, a home of your own. The peace of mind that comes with doing the right thing. I remember being your age," the old man began.

"I didn't think I'd have a chance at marriage. I didn't have the greatest family. But I persevered. Even though they divorced, both of my parents loved me tremendously, and now I realize their intentions for me were good. But it was tough. Many nights I remember lying in bed, thinking, *I'm not going to risk having divorce happen to me. A wife? A family? Why?* I was convinced I would never risk exposing my kids to divorce."

He sipped some lemonade, then continued: "As a teenager, I experienced new emotions. I didn't believe in love, though. I thought it was only infatuation. I had this friend. In eighth grade she had a crush on me. We were afraid to let each other know how we felt, so we just

139

talked. She became my best friend. All through high school we were like peas and carrots.

"She had problems in her family, too. I tried to help her out. I did my best to take care of her. She was smart, and beautiful, too. Other young fellas wanted her to be theirs. And since this is between you and me"—he winked—"I'll tell you I wanted her to be mine, too.

"We tried going out once, but things blew up and we didn't talk for nine months. Then one day in class I got up the nerve to write her a note. She wrote back and things slowly picked up again. Then she went to college."

The old man paused and poured us more lemonade.

"She went to school in Minnesota, where her father lived," he continued. "I wanted to play baseball. I got turned down by college after college—then finally was accepted by a small school, also in Minnesota! It was so ironic. When I told her, she cried.

"Anyway, we began dating. I remember kissing her for the first time in my room. My heart beat very fast. I was afraid of rejection. But our relationship grew.

"After college, I got to play baseball professionally. Then, I married that sweet girl of mine. I never would have believed I'd be walking down the aisle."

I looked at him, wondering if the story was over. "That's a sweet story. And this is good lemonade, too."

The old man bowed his head. "Thank you. It was her recipe. One of the many, many sweet things she brought to my life. I never take a sip without thinking of her, even though she's been gone for ten years now."

PERFECT PAIR
SIR TEMULJI NARIMAN
AND LADY NARIMAN

In one of history's strangest arranged marriages, five-year-old Bombay (Mumbai) resident Sir Temulji Nariman married the newly dubbed Lady Nariman, who was Temulji's cousin and also only five. Despite the odd beginning, the couple stayed married for eighty-eight years, until Sir Temulji's death, at the age of ninety-three.

Love is the same thing as like,
except you feel sexier.

JUDITH VIORST

A Prayer for Our Journey Together

God, bless to us this day,
God, bless to us this night;
Bless, O bless, Thou God of grace,
Each day and hour of our life;

God, bless the pathway on which we go;
God, bless the earth that is beneath our feet;
Bless, O God, and give to us Thy love,
O God of gods, bless our rest and our repose;
Bless, O God, and give to us Thy love,
And bless, O God of gods, our repose.

Love Booster

Show your true love, in large ways and small, by how much you appreciate him or her.

SWEET CORNCAKES FOR YOUR "SWEETCAKES"

1 14.75-ounce can creamed corn

1 cup yellow cornmeal, divided in half

$^1/_2$ cup water

2 tablespoons olive oil (plus additional oil for
    griddle)

1 large egg

$^1/_2$ cup flour

$^1/_2$ teaspoon salt

$1^1/_2$ teaspoons baking powder

Heat creamed corn in a medium saucepan over medium heat. Stir in half of the cornmeal. Whisk in the water, then the oil, then the egg. In a bowl, mix the remaining cornmeal with the flour, salt, and baking powder. Stir wet ingredients into dry ingredients, until just combined. Heat a griddle to medium, then brush lightly with oil. Drop batter, in $^1/_4$ cup portions, onto the hot, lightly greased griddle. Cook, turning once, until both sides of each corncake is golden brown (about five minutes total). Finish with a dollop of yogurt and some honey or maple syrup.

Reasons Why

Just because I loves you

That's de reason why

Ma soul is full of color

Like da wings of a butterfly.

Just because I loves you

That's de reason why

My heart's a fluttering aspen leaf

When you pass by.

Langston Hughes

Did You Know? At parties, the renowned inventor Thomas Edison and his wife, Mina, secretly communicated with each other by tapping out Morse-code messages into the palms of each other's hands. Edison even used this method to propose to Mina.

In my Sunday-school class there was a beautiful little girl with golden curls. I was smitten at once.

HARRY S TRUMAN
about his wife, Bess

To be in love is to surpass oneself.

OSCAR WILDE

Love is heaven, and heaven is love.

SIR WALTER SCOTT

Till I loved I never lived—enough.

EMILY DICKINSON

Love: When Life Imitates Art

In the world of entertainment, people change spouses about as often as they change their socks. However, many famous couples have bucked the trend and stayed together, despite the myriad temptations and pressures. The website haferbros.com asked respondents to name their Favorite Famous Couples. Below are the top vote-getters. Can you think of others?

Tim McGraw and Faith Hill

Will Smith and Jada Pinkett Smith

Paul Newman and Joanne Woodward

Michael Douglas and Catherine Zeta-Jones

Tom Hanks and Rita Wilson

Brad Pitt and Angelina Jolie

Beyoncé and Jay-Z

Sarah Michelle Gellar and Freddie Prinze Jr.

Diane Sawyer and Mike Nichols

Dr. Phil and Robin McGraw

John Travolta and Kelly Preston

Denzel and Pauletta Washington

Bruce Springsteen and Patti Scialfa

Ben Stiller and Christine Taylor

Kirk Douglas and Anne Buydens Douglas

Sarah Jessica Parker and Matthew Broderick

Billy Graham and Ruth Bell Graham

A Long, Long Kiss

A long, long kiss, a kiss of youth, and love,
And beauty, all concentrating like rays
Into one focus, kindled from above.
Such kisses as belong to early days,
Where heart, and soul, and sense, in concert move,
And the blood's lava, and the pulse ablaze,
Each kiss a heart-quake—for a kiss's strength,
I think must be reckon'd by its length.

LORD BYRON

Did You Know? For more than twenty years "Morganna the Kissing Bandit" snuck onto Major League Baseball fields to plant kisses on unsuspecting players. She even managed to smooch Kansas City superstar George Brett during the 1979 All-Star Game. Morganna didn't abandon her "hobby" until 1999, when she was no longer agile enough to elude stadium security.

Did You Know? In 1967, Kathrine Switzer became the first woman to compete in the Boston Marathon. However, women weren't officially allowed in the famed race until 1972. Thus, during the 1967 marathon, the race director tried to pull Switzer off the course, but her boyfriend intervened and shoved the director aside so that his girl could complete her historic 26.2-mile run. (She entered the race as "K. W. Switzer," so her application raised no suspicion.)

Did You Know? A woman is six more times likely to exercise if her husband exercises too.

Advice

Folks, I'm telling you,
birthing is hard
and dying is mean—
so get yourself
a little loving
in between.

Langston Hughes

To wait an Hour is long
if Love be just beyond
To wait Eternity is short
if Love reward the end.

Emily Dickinson

HERE'S WHAT I LOVE ABOUT YOU...

It's a challenge every person in love faces: How do you tell your true love how much you care—without resorting to the usual clichés?

What follows are several prompts that should help spark some new ways to tell your special someone why, how, and how much he or she is so special.

- When I first met you, you reminded me of...
- If I had to pick three words that describe you best, I'd have to go with...
  1.
  2.
  3.
- By far, my favorite activity to do with you is...
- I knew I was head-over-heels in love with you when...
- If you were a coffee drink, you'd be a _____ , because...
- My favorite "you and me" story I like to tell friends and family is the one about...
- The time you cheered me up most—when I needed it most—was...
- If our relationship was made into a movie, it should be called...
- The thing you do that makes me laugh the hardest is...
- I don't tell you enough how much I value your...
- The trait of yours that I envy most is...
- If we had a theme song, it would be...
- The way you've influenced my life the most is...
- Without you in my life, I would have never...
- My favorite "you quirk" is...

- If I were to make a playlist for you, the ten songs I'd include for sure would be...

  1.

  2.

  3.

  4.

  5.

  6.

  7.

  8.

  9.

  10.

- The animal that most reminds me of you is the _____ , because...

- If we were a dinner-combo entrée, we'd be the...

- The aroma that always makes me think of you is...

- If money were no object, I'd take you to _____ in a heartbeat.

- My favorite photo of the two of us is the one where we are...

- If I wrote a book about the "story of us," I think I'd title it...

- I don't tell you enough that...

- Ten years from now, I can see us...

Love Buster

Say disparaging things about your spouse's family or friends.

A kiss is a lovely trick designed by nature
to stop speech when words become superfluous.

INGRID BERGMAN

Anyone can be passionate,
but it takes real lovers to be silly.

ROSE FRANKEN

The way to love anything is to
realize that it might be lost.

G. K. CHESTERTON

Love grows by giving. The love we give
away is the only love we keep. The only
way to retain love is to give it away.

ELBERT HUBBARD

Let's grow old together—
but as slowly as possible, please.

TAYLOR MORGAN

A Couple's Prayer of Hope

Dear Author of Love,

We know that our love story might take us to many strange and unexpected places, but we thank You that it will *never* take us anywhere that You are not present.

Amen.

Love Booster
Be available, physically and emotionally, when your sweetie needs you.

On Marriage and Mayhem

By Todd Hafer and Jedd Hafer

Our mom and dad were married for almost forty-three years, until Mom's death from cancer. This kind of longevity is admirable under any circumstances, but it's downright astounding when you consider that they raised four boys; served as pastor plus pastor's long-suffering wife in more than a dozen churches; owned legions of cats, dogs, reptiles, and amphibians; and moved seventeen times.

It's not surprising, then, that we heard this question many times: "What's the secret to keeping a marriage together for so long—the way your parents have?"

The answer: Argue. A lot.

We're not kidding. Of course, we should clarify something. A couple must argue about life's most insignificant details. Find the most irrelevant matter and battle over it as if it were the last scrap of beef jerky on a desert island. This way, a couple will lack the desire and energy to fight about the big stuff. This might seem like a strange tactic, but we saw it work for decades. It's kind of like a flu shot—they give you a small bit of a killed virus to protect you from the big, alive-and-kicking Kung-Fu Flu. Think of our parents' method as Preventive Bickering.

Perhaps, though, you've been to too many marriage-enrichment seminars and have forgotten how to quarrel over life's minutiae. Fear not. Using actual examples from Mom and Pops Hafer's forty-plus years of life together, we now present this refresher course in Preventive Bickering. Consider, if you will, the following...

The Horrific Horn Honk Harangue

We had just begun a family trip in our luxury 1968 Dodge Dart when Dad inadvertently bumped the car's horn with his elbow. It was just a tiny honk, but that's all a seasoned couple needs.

Mom: Who are you honking at?

Dad: No one.

Mom: You just honked at *someone*!

Dad: No, I didn't.

Mom: (annoyed silence, followed by...) Kids, did you just hear your dad honk?

Todd: Mom, Dad is not a goose. How could he honk?

Rest of Family (in unison): Shut up, Todd!

Mom: Look, did you kids hear your father honk the horn or not?

All Four Kids (with deep, collective sigh): Yeah.

Dad: So, what's your point?

Mom: So? So! You just said you didn't honk the horn!

Dad: No. I merely said I didn't honk *at* anybody.

Mom (through clenched teeth): No, you did not. You said you didn't honk the horn!

Dad: I never said a thing about merely honking the horn. You asked who I honked at and I said, "No one."

Mom: Kids, did you hear him say...

Jedd (age five at the time): Listen, if the two of you don't straighten up right now, we'll turn this car around and go right back home!

Are you beginning to see the genius in our parents' method? But wait—there's more. The Horrific Horn Honk Harangue is nothing compared to...

The Bombastic Banana Race

One quiet summer morning, the Hafer family was enjoying breakfast. Mom was being the prototypical Proverbs 31 woman, serving her husband by preparing for him a slice of banana bread—the real, low-tech banana bread. You take a piece of bread. Then you slice a banana and put the slices on top.

Mom was using her standard technique, hacking the banana into slices and carefully placing each circular piece on the bread. Unfortunately, Dad was ravenous on this particular morning, and that would prove to be his undoing. For, lo, his hunger drove him to question Mom's technique. The ensuing exchange went like this:

Dad: Not to make a big deal of it or anything, but what you're doing there isn't very efficient. If you cut up the whole banana and then have to position each slice, you're handling every banana piece twice. A better way would be to slice off one banana piece—so it sticks to the knife—then wipe the slice onto the bread.

Mom: You're wrong. My way's much better.

Dad (forcing a laugh): Well, no. It isn't. My way's quicker—I'm telling you. You're just not being teachable.

Mom: Ha! You think you can teach *me* about preparing banana bread?

At this point, our parents did what any two mature adults would do: They decided to stage a race to see whose banana-bread technique was superior. Eagerly, they each grabbed a banana and a naked piece of bread. Jedd had to say "Go!" because he was the youngest, and therefore Dad's threat of "Do what I say or we're going to give the puppy back to the animal shelter!" scared him the most.

So Jedd counted down and Mom and Dad were on their way.

Mom: *Hack-hack-hack-hack. Place banana. Place banana. Place banana. Place banana...*

Dad: *Slice/swipe. Slice/swipe. Slice/swipe. Slice/swipe...*

Mom, always insightful, soon noticed that Dad was edging ahead of her. He had only one more row of bananas to slice and swipe. So, summoning her last reserve of energy, she chopped her remaining stub of banana like a crazed samurai and flung the pieces onto the bread. She struck a blow for women's rights that day. She proved she was a world-class bananathlete. And she handled her victory with quiet dignity.

Mom: I WIN! I WIN! I WIN! HA-HA-HA-HA-HA! Kids, did you see that? I whipped your daddy's hindquarters real good, didn't I?!

Dad watched Mom's celebration with a smug grin, wagging his head. Then he spoke.

Dad: Honey, you didn't win. I'm filing a protest with the commissioner—I mean, the children.

Mom: What? A protest? What are you talking about? I'm done with my bread; you didn't finish yours. Case. Closed.

Dad: Yes, let's talk about my banana bread, shall we? It might be incomplete, but it is neat and orderly. Look at your bread. Look at the way the bananas are carelessly piled up in a big heap. It looks like some kind of crude pagan banana altar. I don't think our Lord and Savior is pleased with that.

Mom: Oh, spare me! You're just a sore loser! I win! Don't I, kids?

Again, the pressure was on the four of us. We conferred briefly.

Jedd: Well, they *both* spank us.

Brother Chadd: True, little brother, but Mom is the one who *feeds* us. Dad hasn't even figured out how to work the microwave after all these years. Every time he tries to heat his coffee, he resets the clock to Eastern Standard Time, but the coffee's still cold.

We all nodded solemnly at Chadd's wisdom.

Todd (with fervor): We've reached a verdict: Mom, you win!

Mom: Whooo-eeeeeeeeeeeeeeeeeeeeeeeeeeeeeeeeeeeee!

Mom jumped to her feet, spiked her banana peel like a football, and did her version of the end-zone dance—making a point to shake her personal end zone in Dad's face. Dad pounded his fist on the table.

Dad: No fair! No fair! I was robbed! This is an outrage.

At this point, the manager of the Village Inn where we were dining arrived at our table.

Manager: I'm sorry, folks, but I'm going to have to ask you to leave. And if you would be so kind...please don't ever come back. I never would have given you bananas if I'd known something like this was going to happen.

We trudged out of the restaurant, dejected. Except Mom. Still giddy with victory, she high-fived a busboy on the way out the door.

So, how did our parents overcome this hotly contested banana fiasco? How did their marriage survive such a controversy? Well, when we got home, they were both so exhausted that they collapsed together on the couch and fell asleep. Mom nestled on Dad's chest. Not a word was said about how the church offerings had been meager lately and that Mom was going to have to start substitute teaching again.

A few hours later, they woke up, smiling sheepishly at each other.

"You hungry, honey?" Mom asked.

"I'm famished, babe," he replied. "You know, I could really go for some of your delicious banana bread..."[5]

Romance Trivia

Romance novels are more popular than ever.

Fifty-three percent of all mass market paperback books

sold in this country are romances. Romance novels

earn more money in the United States yearly

than baseball! So, what's the national pastime?

"LET'S GET SAUCY" SOUTHWESTERN BARBECUE SAUCE

$3/4$ cup chopped yellow or white onion

2 tablespoons minced garlic

2 tablespoons vegetable oil

1 tablespoon minced jalapeño peppers

2 tablespoons Worcestershire sauce

$1/2$ cup tomato paste

$1/2$ cup apple cider vinegar

$1/4$ cup brown sugar

1 tablespoon cumin

1 tablespoon chili powder

$1/4$ cup chopped chipotle peppers

2 cups chicken stock

Sauté the onions and garlic in the vegetable oil until slightly browned. Add remaining ingredients, and simmer for 20 to 30 minutes—until the mixture is thickened to desired consistency. Yield: 1 quart of sauce.

The First Day

I wish I could remember the first day,
First hour, first moment of your meeting me;
If bright or dim the season, it might be
Summer or winter for aught I can say.
So unrecorded did it slip away,
So blind was I to see and to foresee,
So dull to mark the budding of my tree
That would not blossom for many a May.
If only I could recollect it! Such
A day of days! I let it come and go
As traceless as a thaw of bygone snow.
It seemed to mean so little, so much!
If only now I could recall that touch,
First touch of hand in hand!—Did one but know.

Christina Rossetti

Did You Know? In criminal jargon, "getting a valentine" means receiving a one-year jail sentence.

LOVE BY MAIL

Every year the chambers of commerce in a number of cities with romantic names allow people to send their preaddressed, prestamped Valentine cards to them in a larger envelope. These are then given their cities' extra-special postmark and mailed out to sweethearts across the country. If you'd like to send a valentine via this loving route, send correspondence to Postmaster, Attn: Valentines at any of the following addresses:

Loveland, CO 80537
Valentine, TX 79854
Valentine, NE 69201
Kissimmee, FL 32741
Loving, NM 88256
Romance, AR 72136

Love Buster

Compare your spouse unfavorably with a friend or relative you both know.

Cruise Down Memory Lane

What do you remember most about the day you and your sweetheart first met? How about your first date?

For a fun, nostalgic time together, see if you can re-create the moment you first met or your first date. Unleash your memory powers, and try to get the details right, or at least *close* to right. Go back to that same restaurant, or theater, or stadium.

What did each of you wear? If you don't have those clothes anymore (or fitting into them might be a stretch), a close substitute will do. And if friends or family members were involved (e.g., on a double date), why not include them in the fun? Bottom line: whether your trip down memory lane is simple or elaborate, have a great time refreshing your memories of an early chapter in your love story.

Cost: Depends on what happened the first time around. And remember to be creative if cost becomes a challenge or you encounter some other obstacle. For example, if your first date was at a little mom-and-pop diner that's now closed—or five hundred miles away from where you live—find the next best thing close to home.

Make the Date Deluxe: Re-create your marriage proposal. To make the event even more special, you could surprise your loved one with a new wedding band or some other piece of jewelry.

Resources: Beyond your own memory, ask a friend or relative for help in remembering those key details. An old photo album can be a trusty friend as well.

Four Amazing Things

There are three things that amaze me—
no, four things that I don't understand:
how an eagle glides through the sky,
how a snake slithers on a rock,
how a ship navigates the ocean,
how a man loves a women.

PROVERBS 30:18–19, NLT

[God] didn't love in order to get something from us
but to give everything of himself to us. Love like that.

EPHESIANS 5:2

Enjoy life with the wife whom you love.

ECCLESIASTES 9:9, NRSV

Love Ain't No Picnic—Or Is It...

If you haven't enjoyed a scenic outdoor meal with your sweetie in a long while (or ever), it is time to discover (or rediscover) the scenic outdoors. Walk hand in hand, feed ducks or other birds, and enjoy the beauty of nature. Bask in the sunlight and enjoy a delicious sandwich and other picnic goodies.

Cost: Picnic-friendly foods and drinks are also friendly to your wallet or pocketbook. Twenty bucks can buy a lot of crackers, cheese, chips, deli meat, cookies, and soda or juice.

Make the Date Deluxe: Choose an extra-special site for your picnic: a state park, the beach, or some romantic spot that has special meaning for the two of you. Bring a camera and take some pictures to preserve the memories.

Resources: You should be able to find nearby parks and picnic areas on your city's website. For a list of state parks, refer to your state's tourism department, or do a web-search using keywords like *Colorado State Parks* or *public beaches in Southern California*.

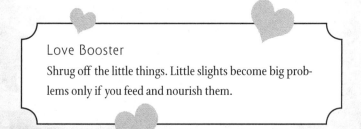

Love Booster
Shrug off the little things. Little slights become big problems only if you feed and nourish them.

Sweetest Fanny,

You fear, sometimes, I do not love you so much as you wish? My dear Girl I love you ever and ever and without reserve. The more I have known you, the more have I lov'd. In every way—even my jealousies have been agonies of Love, in the hottest fit I ever had I would have died for you. I have vex'd you too much. But for Love! Can I help it? You are always new. The last of your kisses ever the sweetest; the last smile the brightest; the last movement the gracefullest.

FROM JOHN KEATS TO FANNY BRAWNE

Did You Know? If you have ever stolen a kiss under the mistletoe, you should thank the ancient Druids. The Druids, a Celtic order of priests, believed the mistletoe plant to be a symbol of peace, so the politically tenuous negotiations between warring Celtic tribes were held under branches sporting mistletoe plants. Under the mistletoe, the negotiators would lay down their arms as a sign of truce. Later, when the Celts converted to Christianity, mistletoe survived as an emblem of goodwill and friendship.

Eventually, mistletoe began to be hung over doorways at Christmastime, and guests were often greeted at these doorways with a friendly kiss or "holy kiss."

The custom continued to morph, and during the eighteenth century in England, it became socially permissible for an unmarried man to kiss any unmarried woman whom he happened to catch beneath the famous parasitic plant.

Ironically, while mistletoe can be enjoyable to kiss under, it should not be eaten. Both its leaves and berries are toxic and potentially lethal.

Falling in Love

Young love-making, that gossamer web! Even the points it clings to—the things when its subtle interlacings are swung—are scarcely perceptible: momentary touches of fingertips, meetings of rays from blue and dark orbs, unfinished phrases, lightest changes of cheek and lip, faintest tremors. The web itself is made of spontaneous beliefs and indefinable joys, yearnings of one life towards another, visions of completeness, indefinite trust.

GEORGE ELIOT

Love Buster

Focus on your spouse's faults, not all those good qualities.

"I RELISH YOU!"
RED ONION RELISH

1 finely diced medium red onion

2 finely diced garlic cloves

$3/4$ cup red cooking wine (or red wine of your choice)

3 tablespoons chopped fresh cilantro

1 tablespoon red wine vinegar

$1\frac{1}{2}$ tablespoons olive oil

1 ounce capers

Salt and pepper to taste

Gently sauté the onion and garlic until tender. Remove from heat and set aside.

In a separate pot, reduce red wine to $1/4$ cup. Combine all ingredients and toss well. Season to your liking. Yield: about 1 cup of relish.

Kissing Trivia

On average, a person will spend two weeks

kissing over the course of a lifetime.

Kissing Trivia

Ancient Egyptians kissed with

their noses rather than their lips.

Kissing Trivia

The Chinese didn't kiss at all until they were

introduced to it by the Western world.

Kissing Trivia

You burn twenty-six calories in a one-minute kiss.

Ten Rules for Having a Great "Us Day" Every Day of the Year

1. Appreciate the value of your time together. Grab it, use it well, and savor every moment possible.

2. Applaud your honey's successes, both large and small.

3. Have a good reason for talking. Have a good reason for remaining silent too.

4. Receive both praise and criticism with grace and patience.

5. Know your true love's pet peeves, and don't invite them in to spend time with the two of you.

6. Remember that it's easier to prevent bad lifestyle habits than it is to break them once they're formed. (Pick up those socks, put the phone back on the charger, return the TV remote to its proper place, etc.)

7. Remember that on life's road, it's not just where you're going; it's who you have beside you on the way.

8. Keep in mind that of all the items you can wear when you wake each morning, your loving smile is the most important.

9. Be real with each other. All the time.

10. Don't forget to say thank you. Your grateful-
ness is not a given, even with the person you're
closest to.

Love is like a mountain, hard to climb,
but once you get to the top, the view is beautiful.

DANIEL MONROE TUTTLE

It's not how much we give,
but how much love we put into giving.

MOTHER TERESA

Love means never having to ask,
"Are you going to finish your dessert?"

GEORGE HOUSE

A heart that loves is always young.

GREEK PROVERB

Paradise is always where love dwells.

JEAN PAUL RICHTER

Give all to love; obey thy heart.

RALPH WALDO EMERSON

'Tis the most tender part of love, each other to forgive.

JOHN SHEFFIELD

*In our life there is a single color, as on an
artist's palette, which provides the meaning
of life and art. It is the color of love.*

MARC CHAGALL

Beating the Heck Out of Romance

By Cindy Sigler Dagnan

The late movie ended. Tana yawned and kissed her husband on the cheek, struggling to get off the couch.

"Go ahead and go to bed, sweetie," she told him. "I'll just be a few minutes more." Brent tugged on her hands, helping her up, then bent down and tenderly kissed her swollen belly.

Swatting him away, she teased, "Hey! Don't kiss the elephant. It'll only encourage her to get bigger."

"I happen to adore elephants, especially when they're as cute as this one. Don't be long."

Tana heard the wistfulness in his voice, but this pregnancy was wearing her out.

Romantic evenings and grand gestures were rare. Besides, it didn't seem like marriage with a baby on the way was very romantic. You went to work, came home and did chores, then flopped on the couch in mindless inactivity. Later you stumbled to bed, too sleepy for anything more intimate than a peck on the lips.

Walking into the tiny combination bathroom/laundry room, she bent awkwardly, picking up dirty clothes to load in the washing machine, a never-ending part of her bedtime routine. She might as well stall; sleep was hard to come by. She just couldn't get comfortable. She sorted clothes. She grinned, thinking about the pastel colors that would soon fill their laundry baskets.

A sudden harsh noise, sounding vaguely like drunken, brawling cowboys, was the only warning. Then, suddenly, the toilet lid flew open, gushing a brown stream of geyser force. And that hideous stench! Drat this old farmhouse anyway, with its temperamental septic system.

"Brent! Brent! Come here, quick!" Tana yelled.

She heard his footsteps pounding on the steps and then saw him round the corner, panic in his eyes as he snapped his jeans. "What's wrong? Are you in—?" He looked behind her and saw the problem. Tana dissolved into tears, and Brent ran out the side door to the septic turn-off. The "drunken cowboys" stopped fighting. The brown geyser slowed to a thin, ugly trickle.

Tana sat on the floor just outside the room, unable to face the mess. Her emotions tumbled like clothes in the dryer, and she began to cry. Brent came in and knelt beside her. "Come on, Tan. Up you go. Both of you. Go straight upstairs to bed. I'll take care of it all. You can't help me, and you shouldn't be around all the bleach and cleaning stuff anyway."

She snuffled her tear-streaked face back and forth across his shirt, nodding mutely. Her sobs turned into sporadic hiccups as she trudged up the stairs. She stood in front of the bank of windows in their master bedroom, watching Brent make trip after trip from the house to the far pasture, lugging buckets of muck.

Tana sighed heavily. It had been her idea to live outside town. She had been the one to fall in love with the quirky farmhouse with its row of hundred-year-old maple trees and sprawling three acres. As soon as she saw it, she could picture their children there, running and playing. Brent had given in only because he loved her. Trouble was, something was forever breaking: a section of plaster and lathe; the newel post on the banister; the rotted section of hardwood by the front door.

She pushed open the adjoining door to the nursery and looked around at the hand-me-down crib, the dresser that had been Brent's as a child, and the beautiful rocking chair that he had stripped, sanded, and stained for her. The pale yellows and blues and the promise of that tiny new life soothed Tana, and she padded back to their bed, falling asleep while Brent continued the clean-up.

Striped sunshine fell across her face. Momentarily confused, she saw that Brent's side of the bed was empty. Throwing on a pair of maternity jeans and a pink smocked top, she went downstairs.

She spotted the floor of the room from the kitchen doorway. It looked amazingly clean and white. Venturing further, she felt her eyes fill with tears. Every trace of the septic explosion was gone. The chrome, porcelain, and tile floor gleamed. Brent had obviously purchased brand-new bath mats and toilet seat covers at Walmart. He knew her well enough to know she'd never use the old ones again.

Hearing Brent's footsteps behind her, Tana turned into his embrace. "Everything look okay, hon?"

"It's better than okay! I can't believe you did this!"

He returned her smile. "I've got the car pulled around when you're ready. I thought I'd take my best girl and the elephant to breakfast."

"It's a deal!" She went back upstairs and smoothed on her makeup and threw her hair on top of her head, coming back down as quickly as possible.

"You can drive," Brent said with a mysterious smile.

"Um, okay." Backing out, Tana realized the reason behind the smile. On the back window of the car, he had written, "Brent + Tana = True Love Forever," with blue and yellow window chalk. He'd even written it backward so she could read it in the rearview mirror.

Putting the car back in park, she kissed her husband firmly. It didn't really matter what the experts said; Brent's way of showing her he loved her beat the heck out of romance any old day.[6]

DELICIOUSLY CORNY
YELLOW CORN BISQUE

Kernels from two cobs of yellow corn (save cobs)

3 cups chicken stock

1 teaspoon diced shallots

1 teaspoon minced garlic

$1/4$ pound of butter

3 tablespoons flour

1 tablespoon sugar

$1/4$ teaspoon turmeric

Salt and pepper to taste

1 cup heavy cream (may substitute half-and-half)

Combine the corncobs and chicken stock in a small saucepan to form a corn stock. (Not to be confused with a cornstalk!) Bring stock to a boil and cook for 30 minutes over medium heat. Strain stock and set aside. Sauté the shallots and garlic in the butter until translucent. Add the flour to make a roux. Add the sugar, corn stock, and corn kernels. Bring mixture to a boil, then decrease to a simmer. Add the seasonings and cook for 15 minutes. Add the cream and increase temperature to bring the mixture to a boil for 5 minutes. Stir constantly. Remove mixture from the heat and strain. Yield: about 2 cups of bisque.

A Prayer for the "Uncomfortable Couple"

Dear God,

We love our comfort zone. The well-known routes around our neighborhood. Our favorite pit stops for frozen yogurt or a cappuccino. The people we understand. The people who "get us." The situations we can control. The stuff we are *comfortable* with. We love it when the rewards are certain and the risks are tiny, if not nonexistent.

We confess that even when we do make the effort to reach out to others, we don't reach very far. We donate to familiar churches and charities—in amounts that don't strain our budget. When we volunteer, we hit the same places as our friends—and usually at the same time. It's volunteering as socializing. And this way, there's always someone else to do the really hard and unpleasant stuff—or to deal with the people who make us uncomfortable. The people who threaten to pull us out of our comfort zone, because they don't look like us, act like us, talk like us, or even smell like us.

God, please show us places in life where we need to step out in love and faith. Where we need to quit making excuses and start making a difference. It might be with a member of our family—someone we need to apologize to or make peace with. Or there could be a need out in our city that we can help with. We might even need to jump on a bus or a plane and serve half a world away.

Whatever the case, please give us sharp eyes to see those limiting lines that box us in—and the guts to step across them. No matter how uncomfortable it makes us.

Amen.

I have learned not to worry about love;
but to honor its coming with all my heart.

ALICE WALKER

Love is the law of our being.

MOHANDAS GANDHI

The Coming of Love

It seems to me that the coming of love is like the coming of spring—the date is not to be reckoned by the calendar. It may be slow and gradual; it may be quick and sudden. But in the morning, when we wake and recognize a change in the world without, verdure on the trees, blossoms on the sward, warmth in the sunshine, music in the air, we say spring has come.

EDWARD GEORGE BULWER-LYTTON

Special Occasion Gift Idea

Instead of buying flowers, plant a rosebush, a shrub, or even a tree in your sweetheart's honor. These can be planted in the yard or even in pots to be placed on the patio, on the porch, or inside the house. Flowers quickly die, but these living gifts say "I love you" over and over again.

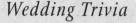

Wedding Trivia

The reason that the engagement ring and wedding
band are worn on the fourth finger of the left hand
is because the ancient Egyptians thought that the
"vein of love" ran from this finger directly to the heart.

SWEET
TRIPLE-CHOCOLATE
ICE CREAM SANDWICH
FOR YOUR SWEETIE

Two 4-inch dark-chocolate chip cookies (cookies can
be homemade or from your favorite bakery)

1 scoop chocolate ice cream

3 tablespoons chocolate sauce

Confectioners' sugar (enough to dust sandwich)

Place one cookie on a serving plate and top it with a scoop
of ice cream. Place other cookie on top and push down
gently. Drizzle sandwich with chocolate sauce—decorating
the plate too, if desired. Dust with confectioners' sugar and
enjoy! Share bites, or make two sandwiches.

A Beautiful Commitment

*Two people who have chosen each other out
of all the species, with the design to be each
other's mutual comfort and entertainment,
have, in that action, bound themselves to
be good-humored, affable, discreet, forgiving,
patient, and joyful, with respect to each other's
frailties and perfections, to the end of their lives.*

JOSEPH ADDISON

*When we hurt each other we should write it down
in the sand, so the winds of forgiveness can make
it go away for good. When we help each other
we should chisel it in stone, lest we never forget.*

CHRISTIAN H. GODEFROY

Give Us Grace

Father God, give us grace for this day.
Not for a lifetime, nor for next week,
nor for tomorrow, just for this day.
Direct our thoughts and bless them.

Romance Trivia

The expression "tying the knot" dates to Roman times,

when the bride wore a girdle that was tied in knots—

which the groom then had the fun of untying.

Did You Know? The term *son of a gun* dates back to the early 1700s. During this era, women were sometimes allowed to accompany their sailor husbands at sea. Pregnancies followed, and it became common practice for a woman to give birth beneath the ship's guns.

Did You Know? Birdseed has replaced rice at many weddings, based on the belief that birds cannot digest rice, or that the rice will puff up in their stomachs and kill them. However, wild birds often feed in rice fields, with no ill effects.

Did You Know? At the 1997 U.S. Women's Open, a prize of $1,700 was offered to the caddie of any golfer who shot a hole-in-one during the tournament. Susie Redman aced a first-round hole, much to the delight of her caddie (and husband), Bo.

Did You Know? Country music legend Loretta Lynn got married (for the first time) at age thirteen. She became a grandma at twenty-nine.

SCORE SOME "LOVE POINTS"

Here's a creative and romantic gift idea for couples in the business world: a PowerPoint presentation that is actually fun to sit through.

First, gather some of your favorite photos of the two of you together—and make sure to include shots of your favorite places. Scan or download your pics into PowerPoint (or other presentation program).

For the text portion of your presentation, include a love poem or lyrics from a romantic song. (If you're really technically adept, add some audio elements as well.)

Conclude by telling your true love that you would be lost without him or her. Allow time for some Q&A—or, better yet—some TLC afterward.

Love Buster
Don't bother to say "I love you." After you've been married awhile, that's a given.

1912

Fraulein Felice!

Write to me only once a week, so that your letter arrives on Sunday—for I cannot endure
your daily letters, I am incapable of enduring
them. For instance, I answer one of your letters,
then lie in bed in apparent calm, but my heart
beats through my entire body and is conscious
only of you. I belong to you; there is really no
other way of expressing it, and that is not strong
enough. But for this very reason I don't want to
know what you are wearing; it confuses me so
much that I cannot deal with life; and that's
why I don't want to know that you are fond of
me. If I did, how could I, fool that I am, go on
sitting in my office, or here at home, instead
of leaping onto a train with my eyes shut and
opening them only when I am with you?

FROM FRANZ KAFKA TO HIS FIANCÉE, FELICE

With Love and Charity

You might be amazed by how meaningful it is to team up with your true love and invest your time, talents, and resources in a good cause. Stand side by side and serve meals at a local soup kitchen or homeless shelter. Enlist sponsors and run or walk for a charity that reflects your values and life priorities. Discover the bonds built and strengthened when two people serve a good cause together.

Cost: In most cases, the only costs involved are time and energy.

Make the Date Deluxe: Consider a short-term mission or relief project, sponsored by your church or other organization. Some churches send a small team of volunteers to a needy area every year. Others deliver Christmas presents to a needy family every holiday season. Participate once and you might make an effort like this part of your Christmas for years to come.

Resources: You won't have to look very hard for volunteer opportunities. Your local church should abound with them. Also keep an eye on the bulletin boards and websites of nearby coffee shops, libraries, and grocery stores. If you have school-age children, you probably already know how desperate schools are for volunteers.

Love Buster
Stay in touch with ex-loves via the Internet.

Hymn to a Good Wife

A good woman is hard to find,
and worth far more than diamonds.
Her husband trusts her without reserve,
and never has reason to regret it.
Never spiteful, she treats him generously
all her life long.
She shops around for the best yarns and cottons,
and enjoys knitting and sewing.
She's like a trading ship that sails to faraway places
and brings back exotic surprises.
She's up before dawn, preparing breakfast
for her family and organizing her day.
She looks over a field and buys it,
then, with money she's put aside, plants a garden.
First thing in the morning, she dresses for work,
rolls up her sleeves, eager to get started.
She senses the worth of her work,
is in no hurry to call it quits for the day.
She's skilled in the crafts of home and hearth,
diligent in homemaking.
She's quick to assist anyone in need,
reaches out to help the poor.
She doesn't worry about her family when it snows;
their winter clothes are all mended and ready to wear.
She makes her own clothing,
and dresses in colorful linens and silks.

Her husband is greatly respected
when he deliberates with the city fathers.
She designs gowns and sells them,
brings the sweaters she knits to the dress shops.
Her clothes are well-made and elegant,
and she always faces tomorrow with a smile.
When she speaks she has something worthwhile to say,
and she always says it kindly.
She keeps an eye on everyone in her household,
and keeps them all busy and productive.
Her children respect and bless her;
her husband joins in with words of praise:
"Many women have done wonderful things,
but you've outclassed them all!"
Charm can mislead and beauty soon fades.
The woman to be admired and praised
is the woman who lives in the Fear-of-God.
Give her everything she deserves!
Festoon her life with praises!

PROVERBS 31:10–31

Let Love Go, If Go She Will

Let love go, if go she will.

Seek not, O fool, her wanton flight to stay.

Of all she gives and takes away

The best remains behind her still.

The best remains behind; in vain

Joy she may give and take again,

Joy she may take and leave us pain,

If yet she leave behind

The constant mind

To meet all fortunes nobly, to endure

All things with a good heart, and still be pure,

Still to be foremost in the foremost cause,

And still be worthy of the love that was.

Love coming is omnipotent indeed,

But not Love going. Let her go. The seed

Springs in the favoring Summer air, and grows,

And waxes strong; and when the Summer goes,

Remains, a perfect tree.

Joy she may give and take again,

Joy she may take and leave us pain.

O Love, and what care we?

For one thing thou hast given, O Love, one thing

Is ours that nothing can remove;

And as the King discrowned is still a King,

The unhappy lover still preserves his love.

ROBERT LOUIS STEVENSON

A Kiss

How delicious is the winning

of a kiss at love's beginning.

THOMAS CAMPBELL

Did You Know? Alexander Graham Bell did not set out to invent the telephone. It was an unintended side-product, springing from the twenty-nine-year-old inventor's efforts to create a device to help his wife and his mom, who were both deaf, hear and communicate better.

In family life, love is the oil that eases friction,
the cement that binds closer together,
and the music that brings harmony.

EVA BURROWS

Smile at each other, smile at your wife,
smile at your husband, smile at
your children, smile at each other.

MOTHER TERESA

Love at first sight is easy to understand; it's
when two people have been looking at each
other for a lifetime that it becomes a miracle.

SAM LEVENSON

To love deeply in one direction
makes us more loving in all others.

ANNE-SOPHIE SWETCHINE

PERFECT PAIR
HUMPHREY BOGART
AND LAUREN BACALL

The chemistry that Humphrey Bogart and Lauren Bacall displayed on the silver screen wasn't only the result of skilled acting. The movie stars fell in love in real life and eventually married. The union lasted twelve years, until Bogart's death. To honor Bogey's memory, Bacall placed a small whistle in his urn. This token was inspired by a line from their first film together (*To Have and Have Not*), in which Bacall told Bogey, "If you need anything, just whistle."

To love or not; in this we stand or fall.

JOHN MILTON

Something Real

By Cindy Sigler Dagnan

"If I had $100, I would buy a real daddy. And that's all."

Nell stood looking at her daughter's answer to that day's school journaling question. Her eyes roamed over the carefully printed, slightly curving letters. She might as well have been holding the pieces of a broken heart.

Blond-haired, blue-eyed Kristie skipped up and tugged on her mother's hand. "Come on, Mama! Let's go! Aren't you done cleaning out my backpack yet?"

Nell smiled and told herself she'd deal with the last-day-of-school cleaning later. She tucked the pink and white gingham bag into a corner of the hall bench. Kristie was obviously eager to get to the carnival in town, and sitting here moping wasn't going to do either one of them any good. She grabbed a light cardigan for each of them from the red hooks by the front door and swung Kristie into her arms. Nell gave her a quick twirl and opened the screen door.

"Come on, *gorgemous*! Last one to the car buys the cotton candy!" Nell said. She set Kristie down, shoved her car keys in her pocket, and scurried down the sidewalk, making sure that Kristie beat her to the car.

"You lose, Mama! I want the pink kind!" Kristie announced as she settled herself into her booster seat. In the rearview mirror, Nell caught a flash of impish grin.

She sighed, wondering why John Brewster had never wanted anything to do with his little girl—with either of them. Six-year-olds could ask tough questions, and Nell had no answers for some of Kristie's.

She sure couldn't quote Kristie's grandpa on the subject of her absentee father: "Worthless no-good. Always was. Always will be."

Once in town, they found Main Street blocked off and lots full of bright lights. Tinny music tinkled out of ancient speakers. The crowd moved in clusters and lines. A group of giggling teenage girls followed by a matching group of guys, trying to act like they weren't interested. Families in line to buy passes for rides and snacks. A few couples, hands swinging between them, headed for the Ferris wheel.

The air was filled with the sweet smell of cotton candy, the salty smell of popcorn and giant pretzels, and the rich aroma of funnel cakes.

"What do you want to do first, sweet girl?" Nell asked.

"I wanna eat a hot dog with mustard and some cotton candy."

"That's what I like: a girl who knows her mind."

Suddenly, Nell and Kristie both turned around and found themselves face to face with Nell's first love, Jared Armstrong.

"What are you—?"

"When did you—?"

Nell and Jared offered their questions almost in unison.

"Ladies first," Jared said, as he made a gallant mock bow.

"Um, things didn't exactly work out, so Kristie and I are back here. Home is always where you end up, you know. What about you?"

"Just home from Iraq and vowing I'd take out the first pretty girl I laid eyes on. Lucky me, here's two of them." He bent down to solemnly shake Kristie's hand. Kristie shook Jared's hand boldly.

Nell marveled at what was happening. In the space of a heartbeat, Jared had swooped back into her life. She watched Jared scoop up Kristie and place her on his shoulders. Kristie sat there, beaming, as if this was exactly where she belonged.

"If you'll do me the honor, I'd like to buy you girls all the hot dogs you can eat and then check out the fair from the top of the Ferris wheel." Jared looked at Nell for permission. "Come on, it'll be just like old times."

"That's right," Kristie chirped. "You used to take Mama to the end-of-school carnival every year. She told me about it, and I saw the pictures in her yearbook. I don't have a yearbook yet, 'cause I'm only just six."

Nell looked up at Kristie and sighed. *Traitor. No one who has kids gets to keep secrets.*

"We're the ones who'd be honored, Jared." Nell said, giving up all effort to hide her delight. "Welcome home," she added softly.

Jared hooked one hand around Kristie's leg to hold her steady and linked his other one through Nell's. They devoured three hot dogs each, plus cotton candy and what seemed like a gallon of Coke over finely crushed ice. They rode the merry-go-round, the Tilt-a-Whirl, and the Kiddie Koaster.

They sat on a bench and watched Kristie ride the children's train, reminiscing about old times and catching up on current times.

"I'm sorry I left to join up without making you promise to wait for me," Jared said. "If I had, John Brewster wouldn't have had a chance, and you would have gotten something real." He looked at Kristie, and his face softened. "But you have her."

"Yes." Nell's mouth was dry. "I'm thankful for her. Nothing like parenting to keep you grounded."

"I bet. She's a great girl." Jared's eyes searched Nell's intently. "Takes after her mama."

He leaned in for the briefest, sweetest kiss, ending it as soon as he heard the train stop.

Kristie clambered onto his lap. "I saw you kiss my mama. If I had a hundred dollars, I think I'd pick you."

Jared looked puzzled. Nell blushed, from her face to the bottom of her feet.

"Maybe I'll explain some other time," she managed.

"It's just that that's how I said I'd spend my money that we wrote about in our journal today," Kristie explained. "I said I'd buy a real daddy."

"Aha." A lump formed in Jared's throat. "Let's get you and your mama home, and maybe we can talk about that hundred dollars over pizza after church on Sunday."

Jared walked them back to the car, a sweet little girl and his best friend from long ago, one on either side of him. Nell could tell that this time, things were different. From the car window, she waved to him, with hope in her heart...and a craving for pizza.[6]

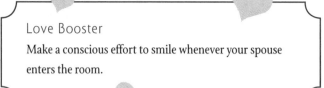

Love Booster

Make a conscious effort to smile whenever your spouse enters the room.

Nothing is sweeter than love,
Nothing is stronger,
Nothing higher,
Nothing wider,
Nothing more pleasant,
Nothing fuller nor better
in heaven and earth.

THOMAS À KEMPIS

I'm a hopeless romantic! When
I'm in a healthy relationship, I'm
more secure, I'm more alive, I'm more
challenged, I'm more...open.

GINNIFER GOODWIN

A Couple's Prayer for Today

Lord, show us Your way. Lord, lead us to Your destination.
We thank You for being our beacon of hope,
a beacon we can always see, if we will only look.

Amen.

Kissing Trivia

You use only two muscles on your face when you give
a peck kiss, but you use all of your facial muscles and
burn more calories during a passionate kiss.

Kissing Trivia

Our brains have special neurons that help us
find each other's lips in the dark.

TANTALIZING
TERIYAKI MAHIMAHI

2 mahimahi filets (about 7 ounces each)
2 thick slices of fresh or canned pineapple
$\frac{1}{2}$ cup teriyaki glaze
2 cups assorted veggies (to stir-fry)
$1\frac{1}{2}$ cups cooked white rice
3 tablespoons orange juice
1 teaspoon orange peel

Grill the mahimahi and the pineapple slices, basting with half of the teriyaki glaze. Stir-fry the veggies with the remaining teriyaki. Pour the veggies onto two plates, and top each with a mound of rice. Combine the orange juice and orange peel, then drizzle onto the rice. Place the fish on the rice, and garnish with pineapple slices.

*Keep your eyes wide open before marriage,
half shut afterwards.*

BENJAMIN FRANKLIN

*I want my husband to take me in his arms and
whisper those three little words that all women long to hear:
"You were right."*

KELLY SMITH

A little kiss can make a big difference.

CYNTHIA LEWIS

*The key to a happy marriage is spending more time
counting blessings than counting troubles.*

REV. JERRY SPRINGSTON

TODAY IS THE FIRST DAY OF THE REST OF YOUR RELATIONSHIP!

Do any of these statements sound familiar to you?

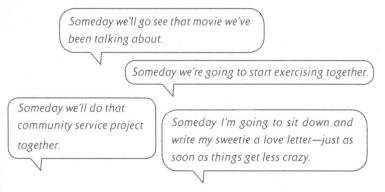

Someday we'll go see that movie we've been talking about.

Someday we're going to start exercising together.

Someday we'll do that community service project together.

Someday I'm going to sit down and write my sweetie a love letter—just as soon as things get less crazy.

Good intentions are fine, but there is a problem with "someday" statements: Sometimes, someday never comes. Opportunities disappear. Movies vanish from theaters. That "interesting new restaurant" closes. The money set aside for the "romantic getaway" gets eaten up by other "priorities."

Heaven knows that life can be busy. But it's your life, and it's up to you how you will spend it. Don't let opportunities to reach out and touch the life of your true love slip through your fingers.

Make an effort. Set priorities. Give yourself some time limits if you must. Write that love letter or e-mail. Order those flowers. Write on that Facebook wall. Buy that gift. Put your names on that "volunteer" list—get committed.

Don't look at time as a prison. Think of it as a gift for two. Then, as you sort through your life's priorities, decide how you want to use this gift of time. Are you going to seize those opportunities to feed and care for your relationship? Or will you let them get away?

Did You Know? Here's a sign of our technology driven times: in a survey, more than 65 percent of respondents said they had been asked out on a date via text message.

Did You Know? At the age of fifty-three, Geraldine Wesolowski actually gave birth to her own grandson. She was implanted with an egg from her daughter-in-law that was fertilized by her son. She carried the baby to term as a literal labor of love.

Did You Know? In Denmark, a lovelorn young man faced jail time when he was unable to pay a $117,000 phone bill—resulting from long-distance calls to his girlfriend in Madras, India. One of the calls lasted twenty-one hours.

Did You Know? Mae West and W. C. Fields, romantic costars of the 1939 film *My Little Chickadee*, despised each other in real life. To the careful observer of the movie, the animus is palpable in some of their scenes together.

Our Perfect Day

For memory has painted this perfect day
With colors that never fade,
And we find at the end of a perfect day
The soul of true love we've made.

AUTHOR UNKNOWN

What Love Is

What love is, if thou wouldst be taught,
Thy heart must teach alone—
Two souls with but a single thought,
Two hearts that beat as one.

FRIEDRICH HALM

A Few Guidelines for Romance in the Digital Age

- If you're tempted to make regular e-contact with an ex-love, ask yourself how you would feel if your significant other was doing the same thing.

- With the first guideline in mind, remember that it's okay to ignore someone who attempts to "friend" you on a social-networking site. It doesn't mean you're a snob; it means you are setting wise boundaries.

- Before you send a romantic e-mail from work, remember that anything created on a work computer is technically the company's property. Moreover, there's the chance that your boss or a coworker might accidentally get cc'd on an e-mail. Finally, if you're in the habit of sending e-mails that are a little spicy or deeply personal, note that certain words or phrases can draw the attention of a company's IT and/or human resources department.

- In today's digital age, a new object of your romance probably knows you will Google him/her in the early stages of your dating life. But be careful about bringing up what you've learned online. It might not be accurate. It might be too personal. And it might be so obscure that you could come off sounding like a stalker. ("I know you attended preschool at Early Harvest First Start Academy decades ago. What kind of snacks did they serve there?")

- If you're listening to your iPod when you encounter your honey, the earbuds need to come out. (Don't just turn off the device or lower the volume.) Show "Sweetie" that you value him or her by giving your full attention. The same advice applies to your Bluetooth.

- Whether you're out for dinner, coffee, drinks, or whatever, don't ignore your date or spouse by constantly checking your PDA or cell. If you truly need a few minutes to review an important e-mail or text, excuse yourself for a moment. But don't let yourself get lost in the "BlackBerry prayer" at the expense of that charming person sitting across from you. It doesn't matter if you've been together ten weeks or twenty-five years, good manners are always a good idea.

*There is no difficulty that enough love will not
conquer; no disease that enough love will not heal;
no door that enough love will not open; no gulf
that enough love will not bridge; no wall that
enough love will not throw down; no wrong
that enough love will not set right.*

EMMET FOX

*The highest level of sexual excitement is
in a monogamous relationship.*

WARREN BEATTY

Did You Know? For centuries, people have in-
gested various things in search of the ultimate love potion. One current fad is extract
of rhinoceros horn. However, a rhino's horn is
merely a hard-packed compound of hair and
keratin—basically the same stuff your finger-
nails are made of.

Love, in a Beautiful Shade of Green

Your mission for this date: Embark on the most ecologically gentle lunch date you can imagine. In other words, step out, but leave a tiny carbon footprint in the process. A simple way to go green is to plan a walk or bike ride to a nearby picnic area. Prepare and pack a lunch, doing your best to ensure that everything (from food to utensils to packaging) is recyclable, reusable, compostable—or a combination of the three. If your destination is a local park, you might find that bins for various recyclables have been provided.

Cost: Depends on what you bring, but you might be surprised to find that going green can save you a lot of green.

Make the Date Deluxe: Go pre-picnic shopping together. See who can find food with the most environmentally friendly packaging and the "greenest" utensils and containers. For a variation on this theme, look for a concert or other performance that benefits an environmental cause. If you can, walk, bike, or carpool to the event. Or use public transportation.

Resources: Look for eco-events in your local paper. As for date ideas, your local library should have a growing list of books on the subject. The aptly titled *The Green Book* is a great place to start. And chances are, you have a friend or relative who is a known eco-warrior. Ask for an idea or two—and you're likely to come away with a bushel!

Love Buster
Assume your spouse doesn't need anything special for birthdays, anniversaries, etc.

The ultimate test of a relationship
is to disagree but to hold hands.

ALEXANDRA PENNEY

A happy life is simply the sum
of many small, happy moments.

PENNY KRUGMAN

Here's a marriage tip: Don't diet together.
Two people should never be that cranky simultaneously.

DREW CODY

You know you've been married a long time
when you start turning off the lights for
economic reasons rather than romantic ones.

H. J. SPRINGSTON

Love set you going like a fat gold watch.

SYLVIA PLATH

Morning Light

By Mindy Hardwick

Hannah stared in dismay at the half-finished glass panels that lay on the card tables in the church sanctuary. How would she ever finish the stained-glass window before tomorrow's sunrise Easter service? Everyone in the small island congregation was counting on her. The soft lighting of the church spilled through the open windows and onto the church's freshly mowed lawn. In the gardens, tulips and daffodils danced in the moonlight. Hannah loved the Island Community Church. It had been her home since she was a child. Raised on the island, by her uncle and aunt after her parents had died in a small-plane accident, Hannah had found safety and peace at the church. She wanted nothing more than to give something back.

Turning back to the task at hand, she bit her lip. She'd always had a hard time asking for help, and now, once again, she had promised more than she could deliver. "Please, God," Hannah prayed. "Give me the strength to finish this project in time for tomorrow's service."

When Pastor Williams had announced that the church had received a large donation to create a stained-glass window, Hannah had eagerly volunteered to work on the project and supervise a few teens who wanted to help. Hannah enjoyed sharing her talents with others, and the stained-glass project was a perfect opportunity. Over the past two weeks, they had designed the pattern and selected the glass. Hannah taught the teens how to cut the glass and solder the pieces together.

They had spent many hours working, but it had been fun. Only hours ago, Hannah had shooed everyone home. She reassured everyone that she could easily finish up. The glass would be in the window by sunrise. She took a deep breath and looked at the clock. There were still several hours before sunrise. Maybe, just maybe, with God's help, she could finish the job.

She pulled on her safety glasses and picked up a soldering iron. Just as she touched the iron to a red glass piece, she felt a tap on the shoulder.

Startled, she whirled around. She found herself face to face with a tall man with bright blue eyes. "I was looking for my nephew," he said. "I didn't mean to startle you. I'm visiting my sister for Easter. She asked if I'd drive over and pick him up."

Hannah set down the soldering iron. She slipped off her safety glasses.

"I'm sorry," the man said. "I didn't introduce myself. I'm Luke Hansen."

"Hannah Tucker. I think Drew took a ride with Ashley. They've taken a fondness toward each other." Hannah smiled. It'd been fun to watch as the two began a romance.

Luke smiled. "Well, I guess he doesn't need a ride." He surveyed the glass covering the tables. "This looks like a large project."

"Yes." Hannah shook her head. "I mean...no." She flushed.

Luke looked at her, puzzled.

Hannah wiped her suddenly sweaty hands on her pants. Why was it so hard to admit that she had taken on more than she could handle?

Luke picked up one of the glass pieces. He easily inserted it into an empty window pane. "Sorry," he said. "It just looked like it fit. I like to do puzzles, and this seems like a giant puzzle."

Hannah smiled. God had sent the perfect person. It was now up to her to ask for the help she needed.

She spoke softly. "The glass windows are supposed to be finished by the morning. I told everyone I could do it. But now..." She paused and gathered her strength. "I was wrong. I can't do it alone."

Without another word, Luke grabbed a blue denim apron hanging on a small post by the table. "How about I place the glass pieces and you can solder them? We should have this done in no time."

Hannah and Luke worked quickly and easily together. As they worked, Luke told Hannah stories about his work as an architect in Seattle. Hannah told Luke stories about living on the island. All too soon, Hannah found herself soldering the last piece of glass and helping Luke hang the glass in the window.

When the glass was in place, Hannah could see a small band of sunlight coming over the water. She faced Luke and said shyly, "I couldn't have done it without you."

Slowly, Luke reached down. He entwined his fingers with hers. "God answers prayers in mysterious ways."

The rising sun filled the glass panes, and colorful light sparkled over Luke and Hannah.[7]

Love Booster

That household chore your spouse hates? Take care of it yourself, at least some of the time.

LIP-SMACKIN'
SPICY LIME POPCORN

8 cups popped popcorn

2 tablespoons melted butter

1 teaspoon freshly grated lime zest

1 teaspoon chili powder

$\frac{1}{2}$ teaspoon sugar

$\frac{1}{2}$ teaspoon salt

$\frac{1}{2}$ teaspoon ground black pepper

Toss popcorn with melted butter. In a small bowl, mix the lime zest, chili powder, sugar, salt, and pepper. Sprinkle this seasoning mix over the popcorn, and toss gently to distribute evenly.

A "Homemade" Prayer of Thanks

Dear Lord, thank You for our home. We ask that You fill it with Your Holy Spirit. Even when we don't have time to polish and dust and vacuum and tighten every loose screw, may it still shine with Your welcome and love, so that whoever comes in our doors senses that You are present.

Marriage is not a ritual or an end. It is a long, intricate, intimate dance together, and nothing matters more than your own sense of balance and your choice of partner.

AMY BLOOM

"WANNA SPAWN?"
SALMON SANDWICH

1 salmon fillet (about 6 ounces)

Dash of salt and pepper, for seasoning salmon

3 slices of sourdough bread (good quality)

3 tablespoons mayonnaise

2 pieces of lettuce, cut to fit the bread slices

3 thin tomato slices

3 slices of bacon, cooked crisp

Cut salmon fillet to fit bread. Season fish with salt and pepper. Grill salmon to desired flakiness. Toast the bread and spread mayonnaise on each slice. Place the salmon and one piece of lettuce on one slice of the toast. Place a second slice of toast on top of the salmon and lettuce. Place the tomato slices, bacon, and the second piece of lettuce on top of toast. Top with third slice of toast. Cut sandwich in two for sharing. (If desired, sandwich can be secured with toothpicks or skewers.)

Love on the Silver Screen

Do you and your special someone have a favorite romantic movie? One that always moves you, no matter how many times you've seen it? Recently, to celebrate one hundred years of cinema, the American Film Institute unveiled its Greatest Love Stories, as chosen by a panel of actors, directors, producers, film critics, and others from the movie industry. Here is the list, from 100 to number 1.

100. *Jerry Maguire*

99. *Pillow Talk*

98. *The Hunchback of Notre Dame*

97. *Grease*

96. *Barefoot in the Park*

95. *Lady and the Tramp*

94. *Body Heat*

93. *Dirty Dancing*

92. *Porgy and Bess*

91. *Working Girl*

90. *The Bridges of Madison County*

89. *Who's Afraid of Virginia Woolf?*

88. *The Princess Bride*

87. *The Unbearable Lightness of Being*

86. *Notorious*

85. *Love Is a Many-Splendored Thing*

84. *Double Indemnity*

83. *Morocco*

82. *Witness*

81. *The Goodbye Girl*

80. *The Sheik*

79. *Jezebel*

78. *Coming Home*

77. *The Awful Truth*

76. *The Quiet Man*

75. *The American President*

74. *Woman of the Year*

73. *The Ghost and Mrs. Muir*

72. *Roxanne* (1987 version)

71. *Way Down East*

70. *Sense and Sensibility* (1995 version)

69. *Harold and Maude*

12. *My Fair Lady*

11. *Annie Hall*

10. *City Lights*

9. *Love Story*

8. *It's a Wonderful Life*

7. *Doctor Zhivago*

6. *The Way We Were*

5. *An Affair to Remember*

4. *Roman Holiday*

3. *West Side Story*

2. *Gone with the Wind*

1. *Casablanca*

Love Buster

Spend more time at work or with friends than with your spouse and/or family.

All His Heart

No riches from his scanty store
My love could impart;
He gave a boon I valued more—
He gave me all his heart.

Helen M. Williams

Did You Know? Traditionally, products designed to enhance the fertility process have focused on women. However, a new at-home screening test for men was recently developed. The test provides male-fertility levels in about an hour. (Incidentally, about 40 percent of couples' fertility challenges are male related, 30 percent are female related, and the remaining 30 percent are medically unexplainable.)

Did You Know? In 1213, King Ferrand of Portugal was captured and imprisoned by the Turks. The Turks demanded a ransom for the king's release. His wife, Jeanne, refused to pay, as she was bitter about a horrid fight the couple had during a recent game of chess. Thus, King Ferrand spent thirteen years in prison before being released. Checkmate!

Did You Know? Because of its reputation as a love potion, chocolate was condemned by seventeenth-century theologian Johan Rauch as an "inflamer of passions." Rauch discouraged monks from consuming it. He even tried to ban chocolate from all monasteries and other holy places.

Did You Know? During the shooting of the classic movie *Casablanca*, the filmmakers refused to tell star Ingrid Bergman whom she would end up with: her husband or old flame Rick Blaine, played by Humphrey Bogart. "We haven't made up our minds," one executive told her. "We'll shoot the ending both ways."

However, after filming the ending seen in the movie, everyone knew it was perfect. They didn't even bother to shoot the alternate.

The essence of love is kindness.

ROBERT LOUIS STEVENSON

*I wonder what memories of yours will persist
as you go on in life. My hunch is that the most
important will have to do with feelings of loving
and being loved—whoever's been close to you.*

FRED ROGERS

Love does not dominate; it cultivates.

JOHANN WOLFGANG VON GOETHE

*Being deeply loved by someone gives you strength,
while loving someone deeply gives you courage.*

LAO-TZU

Love is like pi—natural, irrational, and very important.

LISA HOFFMAN

Not Alone

By Sharon Norris Elliott

"Aunt Sharon, Grandma's gone." My niece Meloni gently broke the news of my mother's passing. It was 4 a.m. on Saturday, March 17, 2001. Just four days previously, we had secured a hospice nurse to help Momma through what doctors figured were the final stages of her fight with stomach cancer. Of course, no one knew how long that fight would last. Now the sweet nurse met me, standing at the foot of Momma's bed, making all the necessary decisions Meloni could no longer handle.

Sadness settled in with the grim reality, even though Momma seemed to be merely sleeping peacefully. She and Daddy had raised me to understand that death for Christians was actually a joyous promotion to everlasting life in God's presence. Daddy had experienced his graduation a few years earlier, so I knew that he and Momma were now rejoicing together. With that realization, the sadness should have lifted a little, but it didn't. Instead, it turned inward.

I'm alone. The thought hit me in the pit of my stomach. My divorce not quite two years earlier had turned me into a single mother, raising my two pre-adolescent sons. But at least I could call Momma when things got hard. She liked to watch *The Tonight Show*, so I could always count on having someone to talk to, even late at night. Now as I stood looking down on her still form, the emptiness started to overwhelm me. My brother, Nick, had his wife, and my sister, Saundra, had her husband. I didn't have a spouse, and now I didn't even have my mother.

Just then, my pager buzzed. *Who could be calling me at five in the morning?* One glance at the number puzzled me even more. The page was from James, a gentleman I had recently started to date. We'd met through a dating service and talked on the phone several times over the past month. We had met in person just nine days previously. *Why is he calling at such an unusual hour?*

All the details regarding Momma were being expertly handled by the hospice nurse, and I realized I couldn't do anything else until my brother and sister arrived, so I went into the living room and dialed James's number.

He answered his phone on the first ring.

"Hi, James. It's Sharon."

His voice was soothing. "I know your mother passed. I'm here for whatever you need." He heard the question in my silence and continued. "When I called your house and you weren't home, I knew." He hesitated slightly, then continued. "This is probably the wrong time to tell you this, but there's no way I should feel like this if we're not supposed to be together."

Again, I was nearly speechless. "But how?"

"We'll talk later today. Concentrate on whatever you have to do and then call me."

Momma was so organized that by two that afternoon all the major details were handled. All that was left to do was receive out-of-town guests and put together the program for the memorial celebration service. Momma was never still while she was well, and she would not have wanted us to sit around looking sad and moping for the next few days. I had asked James to escort me to a wedding that Saturday evening, and we decided to keep our plans. On our way home, James told me about his morning.

He woke at four, with one thought on his mind: *Call her.* One look at the clock brought a response to that notion. *There's no way I'm calling that woman at four o'clock in the morning.* He tried to go back to sleep. But after an hour of tossing and turning, the urge to call me had remained as strong as ever, so he obeyed. Not finding me home at that hour, his mind went straight to my ailing mother, for whom he and his church prayer team had been praying. He paged me.

God's Word says, "Your Father knows what you need before you ask him" (see Matthew 6:32).

Yes, God knew I'd feel alone when I lost my mother. Before I could even ask Him for help, He nudged James at that precise moment to give me the companionship I needed. Not only was James there for me during that very trying week, he and I were engaged the following month. We married on August 4 of that year.

Contrary to my first thought that March morning, God saw to it that I was not alone.[8]

Love Booster

Before starting an argument, remember that they are easy to begin but hard to end.

PERFECT PAIR
WALLIS SIMPSON
AND KING EDWARD VIII

For England's King Edward VIII, it was love the first time he cast his eyes on American divorcée Wallis Simpson. Amid the turmoil of the Second World War, Edward gave up the throne to marry Simpson, a decision seen as scandalous by the ultra-proper royal family and the Church of England. Despite being ostracized by his family, Edward and Wallis lived happily together for decades, until his death in 1972.

I'm not denyin' the women are foolish:
God Almighty made 'em to match men.

GEORGE ELIOT

A PASSION
FOR CREAMY POLENTA

$3/4$ cup low-sodium chicken broth

$3/4$ cup low-fat milk

$1/2$ cup water

$1/2$ cup uncooked polenta

2 teaspoons olive oil

$1/2$ cup chopped Vidalia onion

3 cups chopped white mushrooms

Salt and pepper, if desired

Bring chicken broth, milk, and water to a boil in medium saucepan. Add polenta, mix well, and then reduce heat until polenta is just barely bubbling. Continue cooking, stirring continuously, for about 12 minutes—until polenta is tender and no longer grainy.

In a sauté pan, heat olive oil over medium heat. Add onion and sauté for 3 minutes. Add mushrooms and continue cooking until mushrooms are softened—about 5 to 6 minutes. Season mushrooms and onions with salt and pepper, if desired. Serve over creamy polenta.

A Love Prayer from Saint Paul

So this is my prayer: that your love will flourish and that you will not only love much but well. Learn to love appropriately. You need to use your head and test your feelings so that your love is sincere and intelligent, not sentimental gush.

PHILIPPIANS 1:9–10

What counts in making a happy marriage
is not so much how compatible you are,
but how you deal with incompatibility.

LEO TOLSTOY

Love is a smoke raised with the fume of sighs;

Being purged, a fire sparkling in lovers' eyes;

Being vex'd a sea nourish'd with lovers' tears;

What is it else? A madness most discreet,

A choking gall, and a preserving sweet.

WILLIAM SHAKESPEARE, *Romeo and Juliet*

Love cannot be forced;

Love cannot be coaxed and teased.

It comes out of Heaven,

Unasked and unsought.

PEARL S. BUCK

Did You Know? William Shakespeare got married at the tender age of eighteen, and the Bard's bride shares a name with a popular contemporary actress, Anne Hathaway. (Incidentally, Shakespeare's Hathaway was eight years his senior.)

Love from the center of who you are; don't fake it.

ROMANS 12:9

Clothe yourselves with compassion, kindness, humility, meekness, and patience. Bear with one another and, if anyone has a complaint against another, forgive each other; just as the Lord has forgiven you, so you also must forgive. Above all, clothe yourselves with love, which binds everything together in perfect harmony.

And let the peace of Christ rule in your hearts.

COLOSSIANS 3:12–15, NRSV

Accept one another, then, just as Christ accepted you, in order to bring praise to God.

ROMANS 15:7, NIV

I wake filled with thoughts of you. Your portrait and the intoxicating evening which we spent yesterday have left my senses in turmoil. Sweet, incomparable Josephine, what a strange effect you have on my heart! Are you angry? Do I see you looking sad? Are you worried?

My soul aches with sorrow, and there can be no rest for your lover, but is there still more in store for me when, yielding to the profound feelings which overwhelm me, I draw from your lips, from your heart a love which consumes me with fire?

FROM NAPOLEON BONAPARTE
TO HIS WIFE, JOSEPHINE

A Cookie Hunt? Sweet!

Your mission for this date: Find the best-tasting cookie in town. Visit local bakeries, the cookie shop at your local mall—anyplace you can think of that makes good cookies. You'll probably want to sample just a bite or two of each cookie, and then take the rest home to enjoy later so that you don't end your date early with an upset stomach! If you can't agree on just one winner, you can each rank the cookies from your favorite to least favorite. This date is especially fun during the Christmas season, when there will be additional holiday selections to choose from.

Cost: Depends on just how many cookie bakers your town has to offer. However, cookies are usually inexpensive. Even at a high-end bakery, a basic chocolate-chip cookie shouldn't cost more than a couple of bucks.

Make the Date Deluxe: Come up with your own original cookie recipe and give it a sentimental (even schmaltzy) name that reflects your personal love story.

Resources: Your local phone directory is a good place to start. However, if you have a friend, co-worker, or relative who is an ace baker, ask him or her for recommendations.

Love Buster
Hold on to grudges, with a death grip. Be a scorekeeper of wrongs.

Did You Know? Sweetest Day, celebrated by many couples as a romantic occasion, was established in the 1920s by a Cleveland candy-company worker who wanted to bring happiness to orphans, the elderly, and others who were often forgotten by society at large. Over time, however, the holiday developed into a secondary Valentine's Day. Today, more than 1.5 million Sweetest Day cards are exchanged annually.

Did You Know? The Christmas custom of hanging stockings has its roots in romance. According to legend, three daughters from a poor family in fourth-century Myra (now Turkey) each wanted to get married. However, their hopes were stalled by their financial status, as none could provide the required dowry to a potential groom's family. Fortunately, Nicholas, Bishop of Myra, heard of the women's plight. Well-known for his good deeds and generosity, Nicholas, under cover of night, climbed onto the roof of the family's home and tossed three bags of gold down the chimney. As fate would have it, the bags landed in some stockings, which had been hung to dry by the fire.

What Is Love?

Ask not of me, love, what is love?
Ask what is good of God above—
Ask of the great sun what is light—
Ask what is darkness of the night—
Ask sin of what may be forgiven—
Ask what is happiness of Heaven—
Ask what is folly of the crowd—
Ask what is fashion of the shroud—
Ask what is sweetness of thy kiss—
Ask of thyself what beauty is.

PHILIP JAMES BAILEY

*A career is wonderful, but you can't
curl up with it on a cold night.*

MARILYN MONROE

WILL THE REAL SAINT VALENTINE PLEASE STAND UP?

Who is the Saint Valentine that inspired an international holiday? The answer depends on whom you ask. The early Christian church boasted two saints named Valentine. According to one theory, the holiday is named for a priest named Valentine who gained notability in the late AD 200s, during the reign of the Roman Emperor Claudius II. Claudius forbade young men to get married because he believed that single men made better soldiers. The priest Valentine disagreed and secretly married many young couples, defying the emperor's orders.

The other Valentine was another early Christian who was known for his friendships with children. This Valentine was imprisoned by the Romans because he refused to worship their gods. The children mourned Valentine's imprisonment and visited him often, tossing loving notes between the bars of his cell window. (This practice might explain why people exchange loving cards, letters, and e-mails on Valentine's Day.) This Valentine was executed on February 14, AD 269, according to several historical accounts.

Love Booster
Leave love notes for your honey, especially on days when he or she might need encouragement.

"SMOOTH OPERATOR" BLUE SMOOTHIE

¾ cup frozen wild blueberries
2 tablespoons chilled acai juice
2 tablespoons fresh lime juice
2 tablespoons agave nectar
Splash of lime-flavored seltzer

Place blueberries, acai juice, lime juice, and agave nectar in a blender. Process until smooth.

Pour into a tall chilled glass and top with a splash of lime seltzer. If desired, garnish with a lime wedge and/or blueberries. Share smoothie with someone special—or double the recipe for two smoothies.

To love abundantly is to live abundantly,
and to love forever is to live forever.

HENRY DRUMMOND

The Eskimo has fifty-two names for snow because it is
important to them; there ought to be as many for love.

MARGARET ATWOOD

You'll never be happy if you can't figure out
that loving people is all there is.

GWYNETH PALTROW

You come to love not by finding the perfect person,
but by seeing an imperfect person perfectly.

SAM KEEN

You know you're in love when
you can't fall asleep because reality
is finally better than your dreams.

DR. SEUSS

The Edge of Love

By Karen Patricia O'Connor

Lydia Barry hadn't been this close to an attractive man since she'd kissed her beloved Wilson good-bye at the mortuary on a Friday morning in July. Yet, here she was, a little over a year later, facing a handsome stranger in the middle of a ballroom dance studio.

"Name's Harvey Middleman," came the introduction. The tall, white-haired gentleman with a neatly trimmed mustache smiled at her. "Pleased to meet you." His blue eyes whisked away her worry. "Thanks for being my partner."

"Lydia Barry. Nice to meet you, too." Her cheeks flushed. For her, at seventy-one, romance was out of the question—she'd had her turn—but maybe she could learn to dance.

Harvey took her right hand in his left hand. "Shall we give it a go?"

Lydia sucked in a breath. Thrusting her shoulders back and holding her head high, she tried to mimic the position she remembered seeing on the television show *Dancing with the Stars*.

"I'll try," she said.

Rollo, the instructor, clapped twice and smiled. "Eyes on me, please."

Harvey frowned. "Mind if we move up front? My hearing's not what it used to be," he confessed.

Lydia nodded and bit back a chuckle. Hearing aids, dentures, cataracts. *One thing or another with these old guys.* That's how it had been with her husband, Wilson. But she hadn't minded. He'd been her one true love.

Harvey guided her to the edge of the front row, his right hand firmly planted on the small of her back. Lydia caught sight of her reflection between a tall, robust man and an apple-shaped woman in the mirrored wall behind the instructor. The soft pink hue of her cheeks brought out the tinge of green in her hazel eyes, and the skirt and blouse she'd selected flattered her figure.

But she didn't feel pretty. More like a dandelion in a patch of new grass, apparently the only one in the room dancing with a total stranger. Rollo had arranged their match by tapping them on the shoulder and putting them together.

Lydia noticed her friend Gloria giggling in the arms of her dance partner, Norman, a chunky man wearing a flowered shirt. She'd been the one to rope Lydia into the lessons. "They'll be good for you," Gloria had said the week before when she enrolled the two of them. "Wilson's gone and he's not coming back. You need to get on with your life."

Maybe Gloria was right. Lydia glanced up at Harvey. This could be a good move. She'd longed to dance whenever she saw couples gliding across the floor at weddings and banquets. She'd sat out more dances than she could count during her fifty-year marriage. Wilson wouldn't budge on that one. "I don't dance. Don't ask me." So she never did.

But today, September 7, was a new day. Lydia was very much alive, and dance lessons were on her calendar for this Monday and every Monday for six weeks. There was no turning back. Or was there? She didn't want to make a fool of herself. She'd make up her mind at the end of class.

Harvey took Lydia by the hand and faced the instructor as Rollo modeled the box step with his assistant.

Lydia giggled and whispered to Harvey, "How about I order a copy of *Dancing for Dummies* first thing tomorrow?"

"Make that a dozen copies." He chuckled as he scanned the room. "We all could use a little help."

The song "Isn't It Romantic?" wafted from the speakers. Lydia recognized the Rodgers and Hart tune from way back. Harvey's right hand encircled her waist, and his touch sent a little shiver up her spine. She tried to squelch it but instead relaxed into this moment of pure bliss. *Yes, it is romantic!*

"We'll lean on each other, okay? I'm a bit nervous myself." Harvey's tender words were just what Lydia needed to hear as they took their first steps. Her chin quivered, and she blinked back the happy tears gathering in the corners of her eyes. Harvey whipped out a neatly folded handkerchief from his pants pocket and handed it to her. His kind gesture cuddled Lydia like a cashmere blanket. She blotted her tears and crumpled the handkerchief into a ball with nervous fingers, then stuffed it into the pocket of her lavender skirt. "I'll wash it and return it to you next week. Is that okay?"

"Oh yes! That means you're coming back. I'm glad."

Lydia's heart surged. "I wouldn't miss it."

Harvey moved to the music again and Lydia followed, feeling God's pleasure as He began turning her mourning into dancing.[9]

Love Buster
In an argument, be sure to say the things that you know will hurt your spouse deeply.

Special Occasion Gift Idea

Want to give a gift that will become a keepsake? Find a great picture of the two of you and have it transferred to a mug, a T-shirt, a Christmas ornament, wineglasses, a key chain, or even playing cards. It's easy, fun, and creates a lasting memento.

Anniversary Trivia

A Taiwanese couple are thought to be the longest-married couple. Liu Yung-yang and his wife, Yang Wan, celebrated their eighty-sixth anniversary in 2003. Second place goes to William and Claudia Lillian Ritchie of Lexington, Kentucky. They were married for eighty-three years.

ZIPPY FIZZ FOR TWO

4 ounces simple syrup (plain or your favorite fruity
 flavor)
2 ounces non-alcoholic champagne
2 ounces sparkling white grape juice

In a cocktail shaker, combine 2 ounces of syrup and
1 ounce of non-alcoholic champagne and shake
well. Strain the mixture into a chilled flute. Top with
1 ounce of sparkling white grape juice. Repeat the
above for second serving. Garnish with a lime wedge
or slice of star fruit and enjoy!

Wedding Trivia

August is the top month for weddings,

with an average of 10.2 percent taking place.

June comes in a close second with 9.9 percent.

Kissing Trivia

A German study on kissing found that two-thirds of people

turn their heads to the right when kissing.

Romance Trivia

Two out of five people marry their first love.

Wedding Trivia

Queen Victoria made white the bridal color of choice

when she wore it to wed Prince Albert in 1840.

To My Dear and Loving Husband

If ever two were one, then surely we.

If ever man were lov'd by wife, then thee.

If ever wife was happy in a man,

Compare with me, ye women, if you can.

I prize thy love more than whole Mines of gold

Or all the riches that the East doth hold.

My love is such that Rivers cannot quench,

Nor ought but love from thee give recompense.

Thy love is such I can no way repay.

The heavens reward thee manifold, I pray.

Then while we live, in love let's so persevere

That when we live no more, we may live ever.

ANNE BRADSTREET

What Truly Counts

When we start to count flowers,

we cease to count weeds;

When we start to count blessings,

we cease to count needs;

When we start to count laughter,

we cease to count tears;

When we start to count memories,

we cease to count years.

AUTHOR UNKNOWN

*Love is the thing that enables a woman to sing
while she mops up the floor after her husband
has walked across it in his barn boots.*

A HOOSIER FARMER

GOD, your God, will cut away the thick calluses on your
heart and your children's hearts, freeing you to love GOD,
your God, with your whole heart and soul and live, really live....

And you will make a new start, listening obediently to GOD,
keeping all his commandments that I'm commanding you today.
GOD, your God, will outdo himself in making things go well for you.

DEUTERONOMY 30:6–9

Love one another deeply from the heart.

1 PETER 1:22, NRSV

The fruit of the Spirit is love, joy, peace, patience, kindness,
generosity, faithfulness, gentleness, and self-control.
There is no law against such things.

GALATIANS 5:22–23, NRSV

She Walks in Beauty

She walks in beauty, like the night
Of cloudless climes and starry skies;
And all that's best of dark and bright
Meet in her aspect and her eyes:
Thus mellowed to that tender light
Which heaven to gaudy day denies.

One shade the more, one ray the less,
Had half impaired the nameless grace
Which waves in every raven tress,
Or softly lightens o'er her face;
Where thoughts serenely sweet express
How pure, how dear their dwelling place.

And on that cheek, and o'er that brow,
So soft, so calm, yet eloquent,
The smiles that win, the tints that glow,
But tell of days in goodness spent,
A mind at peace with all below,
A heart whose love is innocent.

LORD BYRON

Whatever our souls are made of,
his and mine are the same.

EMILY BRONTË

The sweetest reward of your marriage is not what
you get out of it, but what you become because of it.

REV. ROBERT ST. JOHN

Where love is concerned, too much is not even enough.

PIERRE DE BEAUMARCHAIS

In short, I will part with anything for you, but you.

LADY MARY WORTLEY MONTAGU

The sweetest joy, the wildest woe, is love.

PEARL BAILEY

TWICE-AS-NICE RICE BREAKFAST FOR TWO

    1 cup cooked brown rice
    $\frac{1}{2}$ cup fat-free soy milk
    2 tablespoons dried cranberries mixed
        with 2 teaspoons sliced almonds
    2 teaspoons real maple syrup
    1 teaspoon cinnamon

Combine the first four ingredients in a saucepan, and cook over medium heat for about 5 minutes—until thoroughly warm. Transfer mixture to two bowls, then sprinkle with cinnamon and enjoy.

By Accident

BY KIMBERLY FISH

I hadn't planned on telling my future children that I met their mother by accident," Mike said, with a glance at the back end of the borrowed car. Smoke wafted from the dented muffler. "But it looks like that's going to be my story."

"There's not going to be *a story*," said the woman standing in a bridal gown, clutching a handful of lacy fabric with one hand and swatting at a curious honeybee with the other. "But I do have to make it to the church on time. Can I call you later with the insurance details? I promise; I'm good for it."

Mike studied the woman with brown curls pinned to the top of her head—wondering how many brides wore Converse sneakers these days. But then what did he know about what was fashionable? He'd been in Afghanistan for the past three years.

A police car whipped into the intersection and parked at an angle that blocked escape. Traffic was redirected around the collision, and though people were turning their heads to stare, no one seemed inconvenienced by the mishap. Except Mike. And, of course, the bride.

"I'm a firm believer in the state of matrimony," Mike said, hands on the hips of his Class A uniform. "So I'd be happy to let you go on your way; however..."

San Antonio sunshine radiated off the pavement. Mike's sunglasses counteracted the glare and allowed him to covertly memorize the lady who personified the answers to his prayers. Minus the fact she was wearing a wedding dress, of course.

Mike exhaled and finished his thought: "...I get the feeling the police are going to feel differently."

"This can't be happening." The woman nibbled her lower lip. "Raul is going to be so angry that I'm late. He'll stomp around and throw things. Dear Lord, he'll probably tweet about this. My name will be ruined."

Mike's spine stiffened. "I'd think twice about marrying someone with anger issues."

"Please! I'm not going to marry *him*."

A whole litany of possibilities for Raul raced through Mike's mind. "So he's...the wedding planner or something?"

"Photographer," she grumbled. "I've been trying to work with him for years; he's the best. But until he called thirty minutes ago I'd never have dreamed the opportunity was possible."

Mike frowned. "Gotta think Raul would be more flexible—considering you're the star of the show."

She looked at him. "That's sweet of you to say. Not true, but still sweet."

"How could you not be the star? You're the bride. And I have to say it: I'd be grateful to my dying breath to marry a girl like you."

She smiled at him. "That's the nicest thing anyone's said to me in... months. Maybe years."

"Then you need to get out more often. And reconsider your groom."

"If only it were that easy." Her gaze shifted from him to something behind him.

He turned to see the police officer set out safety cones. In seconds, his conversation with the bride would turn to traffic laws, insurance, and fines. He had to act quickly. "Actually," he said, "it *can* be that easy."

"No, I have to go through with this thing. People are depending on me. A whole industry has invested in this day, and if I don't come through for them...well, I don't even want to think about the alternative."

"This day isn't supposed to be about pressure," he protested. He saw the way she clutched her dress, protecting the hem from touching the asphalt. He supported her elbows with his hands. "It's supposed to be about love. The forever kind—where people wait for each other, and forgive traffic bumps. The kind of love that understands when delays happen."

She laughed, but there was an edge to it. "I've waited my whole life to meet a guy who said things like that. Why did you have to drive on my street today?"

The remnants of her laughter circled them like drifting smoke.

"Because we were meant to meet." Conviction gave his words bravado. He nodded toward his father's smashed bumper. "Maybe even by accident."

She appeared to be giving his words serious thought.

"I guess it wouldn't hurt to go for coffee," she whispered.

His hands tightened around her elbows. "But I thought you said people were waiting on you at the church."

"They are. But the photo shoot for the wedding catalog won't take more than a few hours." She offered him her hand. "Hi, my name is Charlie. Can you wait a couple of hours for me?"[10]

CUDDLE-ON-THE-COUCH CINNAMON-SUGAR POPCORN

¼ cup unsalted butter
2 vanilla beans, sliced lengthwise
¼ cup powdered sugar
¼ cup granulated sugar
1 tablespoon cinnamon (good quality)
8 cups popped popcorn
Pinch of sea salt

Heat a small saucepan over low heat; add butter and vanilla beans. Cook over low heat until butter takes on vanilla aroma—about 15 minutes. Strain butter and keep warm. In a small bowl, combine sugars and cinnamon. Set aside.

In a large bowl, toss popcorn while drizzling with the vanilla butter. (For a lower-fat snack, use only half the butter and save the rest to use on toast or muffins.) Sprinkle popcorn with dry sugar-cinnamon mixture, then sprinkle with sea salt. Curl up on the couch, watch a movie together, and enjoy your popcorn. Yield: about 4 servings, so try to save some for a next-day snack.)

YOU KNOW YOUR CORPORATE LIFE IS AFFECTING YOUR LOVE LIFE WHEN…

You refer to dating as "test marketing."

Your Valentine's Day cards feature bullet points.

You mark each wedding anniversary with a detailed performance review.

You refer to marrying off one of your kids as "right-sizing."

You end every "lovers' quarrel" by saying, "Let's take this offline."

You check your BlackBerry for scheduling conflicts with dinner dates.

Your spouse rolls his/her eyes when you whisper acronyms in his/her ear.

Love Buster
Believe that old cliché, "Love means never having to say you're sorry."

My dear Mary,

You must know that I cannot see you or think of you with entire indifference; and yet it may be that you are mistaken in regard to what my real feelings towards you are. If I knew you were not, I should not trouble you with this let-ter. Perhaps any other man would know enough without further information, but I consider it my peculiar right to plead ignorance and your bounden duty to allow the plea. I want in all cases to do right, and most particularly so in all cases with women. I want at this particular time more than anything else to do right with you, and if I knew it would be doing right, as I rather suspect it would, to let you alone, I would do it. And for the purpose of making the mat-ter as plain as possible, I now say you can drop the subject, dismiss your thoughts—if you ever had any—from me forever, and leave this letter unanswered without calling forth one accusing murmur from me. And I will even go further and say that if it will add to your comfort and peace of mind to do so, it is my sincere wish that you should.

Do not understand by this that I wish to cut your acquaintance. I mean no such thing. What I do wish is that our further acquaintance should depend upon yourself. If such further acquaint-ance would contribute nothing to your happi-ness, I am sure it would not to mine. If you feel yourself in any degree bound to me, I am now willing to release you, provided you wish it; while, on the other hand, I am willing and even anxious to bind you faster, if I can be convinced that it will in any degree add to your happi-ness. This indeed is the whole question with me. Nothing would make me more miserable than to believe you miserable; nothing more happy than to know you were so.

In what I have now said I cannot be misunderstood; and to make myself understood is the only object of this letter. If it suits you best not to answer this, farewell. A long life and a merry one attend you. But if you conclude to write back, speak as plainly as I do. There can be neither harm nor danger in saying to me anything you think just in the manner you think it.

Your friend,
A. Lincoln

ABRAHAM LINCOLN TO MARY TODD

The B&B Perfect Getaway

Leave your cares behind and sneak away to a bed and breakfast for a relaxing weekend of romance. Choose an inn that fits your style as a couple: A rustic cabin with a western feel? An elegant Victorian inn with lots of charm and history? Or something else entirely? Whether you stay close to home or decide to go somewhere new and take in the sights while you're away, be sure to reserve plenty of time to enjoy being pampered and to bask in the often-rare luxury of uninterrupted time together.

Cost: A night at a B&B tends to run higher than one at a mid-range chain hotel, but the overall quality of the experience (including a homemade breakfast) more than makes up for the difference!

Make the Date Deluxe: Plan a multiday trip somewhere, perhaps to visit a friend or relative. Find intriguing B&Bs to stay in on the way to your destination. If you really feel like splurging, consider a castle or historic home in Europe.

Resources: To locate a bed-and-breakfast in the United States, bbonline .com is a great site. For bed and breakfast listings worldwide, try bnbchoices .com or bedandbreakfast.com.

Love Buster
In public, let your eyes wander to some attractive person passing by.

Speak to Us, Lord

Speak, Lord, for Thy servants heareth,

Speak peace to our anxious souls,

And help us to feel that all our ways

Are under Thy wise control;

That He who cares for the lily,

And heeds the sparrows' fall,

Shall tenderly lead His beloved ones:

For He made and loveth all.

AUTHOR UNKNOWN

Grow Old Along with Me

Grow old along with me!

The best is yet to be.

The last of life, for which the first was made;

Our times are in his hand,

Who saith, "A whole I planned,

Youth shows but half; trust God:

See all, nor be afraid!"

ROBERT BROWNING

Since love grows within you, so beauty grows.
For love is the beauty of the soul.

SAINT AUGUSTINE

Love is the wild card of existence.

RITA MAE BROWN

I gave her my heart, and she gave me a pen.

JOHN CUSACK (IN THE FILM *Say Anything*)

Did You Know? In the 1800s, doctors sometimes prescribed chocolate for their patients suffering from lovesickness. These doctors claimed that chocolate could cure one's love-lorn pining.

How Do I Love Thee

How do I love thee? Let me count the ways.
I love thee to the depth and breadth and height
My soul can reach, when feeling out of sight
For the ends of Being and ideal Grace.
I love thee to the level of every day's
Most quiet need, by sun and candlelight.
I love thee freely, as men strive for Right;
I love thee purely, as they turn from Praise.
I love thee with the passion put to use
In my old griefs, and with my childhood's faith.
I love thee with a love I seemed to lose—
With my lost saints—I love thee with the breath,
Smiles, tears, of all my life!—and, if God choose,
I shall but love thee better after death.

ELIZABETH BARRETT BROWNING,
"Sonnets from the Portuguese"

Love Booster
Take time to gaze into each other's eyes.

Husbands ought to love their own wives as their own bodies;
he who loves his wife loves himself.

EPHESIANS 5:28, NKJV

My beloved friends, let us continue to love each other since
love comes from God. Everyone who loves is born of God and
experiences a relationship with God. The person who refuses to
love doesn't know the first thing about God, because God is love
—so you can't know him if you don't love. This is how God
showed his love for us: God sent his only Son into the world so
we might live through him. This is the kind of love we are talking
about—not that we once upon a time loved God, but that he
loved us and sent his Son as a sacrifice to clear away our sins
and the damage they've done to our relationship with God.

My dear, dear friends, if God loved us like this, we certainly
ought to love each other. No one has seen God, ever. But if we
love one another, God dwells deeply within us, and his love
becomes complete in us—perfect love!

1 JOHN 4:7–12

*The most precious possession
that ever comes to a man in this
world is a woman's heart.*

J. G. HOLLAND

*On the last analysis then, love is life. Love never faileth,
and life never faileth so long as there is love.*

HENRY DRUMMOND

In marriage, sometimes we submit; sometimes we outwit.

RUTH BELL GRAHAM

I love the idea of there being two sexes, don't you?

JAMES THURBER

*A great spouse keeps your secrets, laughs at your jokes,
and has the wisdom, always, to know the difference.*

REV. ROBERT ST. JOHN

Word Countdown for Those in Love

Six most-important words: I admit I made a mistake.

Five most-important words: You did an amazing job.

Four most-important words: What do *you* think?

Three most-important words: I love *you*.
Runner-Up: Pretty, pretty please?

Two most-important words: Thank you.

One most-important word: We.
The least-important word: I.

Love Booster
Remember that the Golden Rule applies to your honey,
not just to "others."

Special Occasion Gift Idea

Have you ever pored over birthday or special-occasion cards looking for something, anything that might express what you feel for your sweetheart? Consider making your own card. Find a wonderful picture of the two of you. Put it in a border, and glue it to the front of a precut, folded piece of paper. Decorate it anyway you like. On the inside, add the date the photo was taken and what that moment in time means to you.

Romance Trivia

For Valentine's Day 2000, a liqueur manufacturer created the world's largest box of chocolates. The heart-shaped box, assembled in New York City, measured fifteen feet high by fifteen feet wide and weighed some 1,300 pounds. It held the record until November of 2002, when Marshall Fields broke the record with a 2,002-pound box of chocolates in Chicago.

PERFECT PAIR
JOHN AND NELLIE WOODEN

Just a few days before he was to be married to his beloved Nellie, twenty-one-year-old John Wooden lost his life savings ($909.05) due to a bank failure. Only a loan from a friend allowed John and Nellie to go through with their wedding. They celebrated their honeymoon by attending a Mills Brothers concert.

The Woodens established a humble household. John played small-time professional basketball and also taught and coached high-school basketball to make ends meet. The couple lived quietly for a decade—until World War II, when John left home to fight for his country. He returned from military service in the navy, only to see the bank foreclose on their home. Undaunted, he took on multiple jobs at Indiana State University. Wooden served as ISU's athletic director, head basketball coach, and head baseball coach. He also taught several classes and completed his master's thesis.

Three years later, Wooden took a job at UCLA, where he became a coaching legend, leading the

Bruins to ten national championships, including seven in a row. Nellie was a constant source
of support and love, and she took the lead in caring for the couple's two children during the hectic
basketball seasons.

All told, John and Nellie were married for almost
fifty-three years, until the latter's death in 1985.
However, her passing didn't dim John's love for
her. On the twenty-first day of every month (she
died on March 21), he visited her gravesite and
also wrote her a love letter. Coach Wooden kept
up this monthly labor of love for almost twenty-
five years—the letters piling up in the couple's
home—until his deteriorating health and failing
eyesight got the best of him. But the love in his
heart remained strong, until he died in 2010, just a
few months short of his hundreth birthday.

Marriage: The Tie That Binds

A Reminiscence by Todd Hafer and Jedd Hafer

When we were young kids, the same scenario would play itself out every Sunday morning. Our dad, a minister, would scour the house for some article of clothing, eventually announcing, "I've looked everywhere, and my _____ is nowhere to be found!"

Then, our mom, in her trademark subtle way, would note that if indeed Pastor Hafer had looked *everywhere*, he surely would have found the missing garment. Because it had to be *somewhere*.

We were always impressed by Mom's patience. After all, there was no good reason Dad couldn't find items in his wardrobe. This was the late 1970s, when many of his multicolored polyester ties, shirts, and pants (not to mention his white fake-leather belts) could be detected from outer space.

Mom never scolded Dad. She would just smile, reach into his closet, and then produce the item in question.

"Is this the green-and-orange striped tie with the periwinkle giraffes along the border that you were looking for?" she would ask cheerfully.

"That's it!" came Dad's response. "Where in the wide world of sports did you find it!?"

"Oh, in this strange and wonderful hiding place we like to refer to as 'the closet,' on what is known in some parts of the United States as the 'tie rack.'"

"Huh," Dad would shrug. "I looked there. Twice."

"What do you suppose, honey, is the difference between *your* looking and *my* looking?"

"Uh...men lack women's visual acuity?"

Clearly, Dad was out of his element. Mom, of course, had the real answer: "Men don't really look for things. The rods and cones of their eyes don't truly engage with the correct portion of the brain—the one called 'the brain.' Women, on the other hand, really, really see things. Like ties and messes, and messy ties, and bread crumbs on the counter, full garbage bins begging to be emptied, piles of towels and underwear on the floor, and so on. We women see so many things that actually hurt our eyes. Meanwhile, men don't even seem to notice."

We'd like to pretend that Dad was the only can't-find-his-own-clothes culprit in the Hafer household, but that would be dishonest and misleading. (And also deceptive.) Beyond all that, it just wouldn't be true—so we won't make such claims. In the world of lost and missing clothing, we kids were just as bad as Dad.

For example, our brother Chadd misplaced his wardrobe almost as often as his father did. And like Dad, he would complain to our mom that a given item had "simply disappeared."

"Really?" Mom would say. "Aren't those your dress socks that your brothers are using to play flag football with in the front yard? And isn't that your Sunday-school tie around your head as part of some commando outfit? And, by the way, why is the dog wearing your boxer shorts?"

You know, writing this reminiscence gave us a deep, deep appreciation for the way that the wives/moms of the world keep their families organized, how their keen sense of observation saves everyone from hours of fruitless searches—and from the expense of buying replacement clothes for the ones that are supposedly missing in action.

In fact, our feelings of appreciation grew so strong that we wrote an epic poem of tribute to all the wives/moms of the world. The locators of lost loafers. The miners of misplaced mittens. The finders of forsaken flip-flops. It was a stirring poem. We know that scores of women would post it proudly on their Facebook pages. It would be made into plaques, quilts, and refrigerator magnets. Women would recite it from memory at Bible studies and Bunko games.

Yes, it would touch so many lives...if only we could find it. We wrote it on a napkin—or maybe the back of last week's church bulletin. In any case, it was right around here somewhere, just a few minutes ago. We'd ask our wives about it, but they are away on a church retreat. Sure, they left the phone number of the retreat center, but that number was written on the same napkin (or perhaps church bulletin) that sported the poem. Also, neither one of us can find the phone right now. And we've looked *everywhere* for 'em...[5]

Love Booster
Remind your honey of favorite moments together.

ONE HONEY OF A SALAD WITH SWEET POPPY-SEED DRESSING

Dressing Ingredients

$1/2$ cup honey

2 tablespoons poppy seeds

$3/4$ cup vegetable oil

$1/2$ cup cider vinegar

$1/4$ teaspoon pepper

Salad Ingredients

1 head romaine lettuce, cut up

1 cup pecan halves

1 diced Fuji apple

$1/2$ cup dried cranberries

6 ounces feta cheese, crumbled

1 small red onion, thinly sliced

Combine dressing ingredients in a shaker bottle and mix well. Assemble salad ingredients in salad bowl, and toss with dressing just before serving.

Notes

1. *The Blue Dress* was written by Beatrice Fishback of Suffolk, England. Used by permission of the author.

2. *Candidate for Love* was written by Joan Banks of Joplin, Missouri. Used by permission of the author.

3. *Love at First Sight* and *More Than a Heart Can Hold* were written by Vicki J. Kuyper of Phoenix, Arizona. Used by permission of the author.

4. *If Loving Means I'm Wrong, I Don't Wanna be Right* was written by Jedd Hafer of Colorado Springs, Colorado. Used by permission of the author.

5. *On Marriage and Mayhem* and *Marriage: The Tie That Binds* were written by Todd Hafer of Kansas City, Kansas, and Jedd Hafer of Colorado Springs, Colorado. Used by permission of the authors.

6. *Beating the Heck Out of Romance* and *Something Real* were written by Cindy Sigler Dagnan of Oronogo, Missouri. Used by permission of the author.

7. *Morning Light* was written by Mindy Hardwick of Lake Stevens, Washington. Used by permission of the author.

8. *Not Alone* was written by Sharon Norris Elliott of Englewood, California. Used by permission of the author.

9. *The Edge of Love* was written by Karen Patricia O'Connor of Watsonville, California. Used by permission of the author.

10. *By Accident* was written by Kimberly Fish of Longview, Texas. Used by permission of the author.

Index